The Essential Speaking and Listening

Talk is the medium through which children learn; and yet children may not realise why their contributions to classroom talk are so important. This book provides teachers with resources for developing children's understanding of speaking and listening, and their skills in using talk for learning.

The Essential Speaking and Listening will:

- help children to become more aware of how talk is valuable for learning
- raise their awareness of how and why to listen attentively and to speak with confidence
- encourage dialogue and promote effective group discussion
- integrate speaking and listening into all curriculum areas
- help every child make the most of learning opportunities in whole class and group work contexts.

The inclusive and accessible activities are designed to increase children's engagement and motivation and help raise their achievement. Children will be guided to make the links between speaking, listening, thinking and learning and through the activities they will also be learning important skills for future life.

Teachers, education students and teacher educators will find a tried-and-tested approach that makes a difference to children's understanding of talk and how to use it to learn.

Lyn Dawes is Senior Lecturer in Education at Northampton University, a visiting lecturer at Cambridge University and an experienced teacher. Her work on speaking and listening has been included in guidance for teachers by the National Strategies.

For Emma, Gregory, Auden, Cerelia and Seraphina

The Essential Speaking and Listening

Talk for Learning at Key Stage 2

Lyn Dawes

Illustrated by Lynn Breeze

Routledge
Taylor & Francis Group

LONDON AND NEW YORK

First published 2008
by Routledge
2 Park Square, Milton Park, Abingdon, Oxon OX14 4RN

Simultaneously published in the USA and Canada
by Routledge
270 Madison Ave, New York, NY 10016

Routledge is an imprint of the Taylor & Francis Group, an informa business

Text © 2008 Lyn Dawes

Illustrations © 2008 Lynn Breeze

Typeset in Times New Roman PS by
Florence Production Ltd, Stoodleigh, Devon
Printed and bound in Great Britain by
Bell & Bain Ltd, Glasgow

British Library Cataloguing in Publication Data
A catalogue record for this book is available from the British Library

Library of Congress Cataloging in Publication Data
Dawes, Lyn.
    The essential speaking and listening: talk for learning at key stage 2/
Lyn Dawes.
        p. cm.
    1. Oral communication – Study and teaching – Great Britain.
2. Listening – Study and teaching – Great Britain.   3. Group work
in education – Great Britain.   I. Title.
LB1572.D39 2008
372.62'2—dc22   2007044383

ISBN10: 0–415–44962–6 (pbk)
ISBN10: 0–203–92788–5 (ebk)

ISBN13: 978–0–415–44962–5 (pbk)
ISBN13: 978–0–203–92788–5 (ebk)

Contents

Acknowledgements

I am grateful to all staff and children at Middleton Primary School for their enthusiasm for Thinking Together, especially Jo Clay, Nicola Fisher, Donna Tagg and Jonathan Wilson, Sam, Warwick, Grace and Fritzie. Similarly my colleagues at the University of Bedford and the University of Cambridge, especially Barbara Leedham, Chris Rix, Elaine Wilson and Joan Dearman. I have been privileged to work with many students, now teachers themselves, who have taken the idea of raising children's voices to heart. Particular thanks to Rita Kidd and Darrel Fox. I am extremely proud to be associated with children's raised achievement and growing confidence as reported by Janet Baynham, Literacy Advisor for Newport.

My colleagues at the University of Northampton have helped me by putting ideas into practice with astonishing panache; and by offering well-informed help with early drafts. Thank you Babs Dore, Linda Nicholls and Peter Loxely.

This book is enriched by contributions freely given by a range of eminent professionals in the field of education. Some will appear in a further volume but I would like to thank everyone now for their insightful ideas and their generosity with time. Thank you to Janet Baynham, Babs Dore, Harry Daniels, Linda Bartlett, Vikki Gamble, Prue Goodwin, Liz Grugeon, Claire Sams and Rupert Wegerif. Especial thanks to Douglas Barnes for your lecture extract.

My colleagues on the Thinking Together team have always been an inspiration and invariably offered support and a conviction which I have found immensely helpful. This book is infused with their ideas and would not exist without them. I am indebted to Rupert Wegerif, Judith Kleine Staarman, Karen Littleton, Claire Sams, and Neil Mercer; also my Dialogic Teaching in Science colleagues Phil Scott and Jaume Ametller.

Thank you to my mates Claire, Andrew, Chris, Tara, and Babs for their resilient friendship and all the times they have listened and helped me to keep writing.

My family have provided me with constant input and the most brilliant distractions. Thank you to Derwent, Betsy, Poppy, Emma, Greg, Auden, Cerelia, Mum – and Anna, who has been around all the time while this book has been written and who has recently begun to tell me to switch off the computer and go and do something else.

My husband Neil provides me with open access to his ability to see through muddled phrases and come up with neat ways of putting things. His intellectual generosity means that I have had the unique privilege of discussing anything and everything about the book at any time with a world expert in the field. I have been utterly reliant on this on-tap source of knowledge and his profound understanding which has time and again kept Thinking Together right and true.

Lyn Dawes
24 February 2008

Introduction
Speaking and listening for thinking and learning

> Thought development is determined by language; [. . .] the child's intellectual growth is contingent on mastering the social means of thought, that is, language.
>
> (Lev Vygotsky 1994: 46)

About this book

The Primary Framework for Literacy has opportunities for speaking, listening, group work and drama integrated throughout its Units of Study. However, children unused to thinking aloud with others, or unaware of the importance of talk for learning, may not benefit as fully as they might from such planned opportunities for classroom talk. Teaching speaking and listening for learning enables children and teachers to generate a talk-focused classroom in which all understand the meaning and importance of key phrases such as 'talk together to decide . . .', 'work with your group . . .', 'listen to your partner . . .' 'discuss what you are going to do . . .', and 'think together to decide . . .'.

The activities in this book offer children an understanding of how they learn in classrooms. They gain insight into what is really happening in whole-class sessions and in group work. They develop shared strategies for collaboration through talk. The hidden ground rules which govern learning and profoundly affect the achievement of all learners are brought out for reflection and discussion.

In 2006 Jim Rose, former Ofsted Director of Inspection, completed his independent review of the teaching of early reading. He noted that:

> The indications are that far more attention needs to be given, right from the start, to promoting speaking and listening skills to make sure that children build a good stock of words, learn to listen attentively and speak clearly and confidently. Speaking

and listening, together with reading and writing, are prime communication skills that are central to children's intellectual, social and emotional development.

(Rose 2006)

The activities in this book offer children an essential grounding in effective talk for learning. This is essential for ensuring that children benefit fully from our teaching of language and literacy.

Teachers

Teachers are often judged to be the root cause of things that are wrong in schools or children. As Michael Fullan (Professor Emeritus of the Ontario Institute for Studies in Education of the University of Toronto) says:

If a new program works teachers get little of the credit. If it fails they get most of the blame.

(Fullan 1982: 107)

In reality, the complex, organic places that are schools are influenced by very many factors; and our children are influenced – educated – by their life experiences, not just school. Teachers have a vocation to educate, to help children think, develop, learn and understand. Their success cannot be simply assessed by measuring attributes of their pupils' literacy or numeracy. However, people are always trying to change teachers. This book aims to support and encourage the work of teachers, without wishing to imply a deficit model in which teachers are regarded as essentially and permanently in need of 'development'.

The direct teaching of speaking and listening: talk, listen, think, learn

The primary psychological 'tool for thinking' is language. As well as helping children to acquire a tool for thinking, interaction through spoken language provides children with access to knowledge and new ways of thinking. In order to develop to their full potential, children need to be taught that in classroom contexts, both speaking and listening are to do with learning. They need to know why it is so crucial that they develop their oral language competence and how to do so. They need to see the sort of progress they are making so that they can feel as proud of becoming an articulate speaker as they are of becoming an independent reader or fluent writer.

Higher order thinking and the teaching of speaking and listening

Some ways of thinking require deeper reflection; these ways of thinking – analysis, synthesis (creative thinking) and evaluation – can be described as 'higher order thinking' (Bloom 1956). Such thinking allows a rational, critical approach to solving problems or considering experience. This is what we want children to develop in our classrooms. A fundamental aim for teachers is to help children become aware of their capacity to use their minds for higher order thinking. We can use dialogue and discussion to draw on knowledge and understanding, and encourage opportunities for analysis and creativity. In addition, children can use speaking and listening to reflect on and evaluate their own learning and that of others.

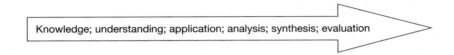

Knowledge; understanding; application; analysis; synthesis; evaluation

Bloom's Taxonomy of Thinking

Deep and surface learning

Roger Säljo, Professor of Pedagogy at Gotenburg University, considers that if we are to understand the way children use higher order thinking, we must find out what language they are using for thinking. Säljo (1979) identifies the ways that people approach learning as 'deep' or 'surface', reflecting not just the intention of the child as a learner, but the kind of understanding they are likely to achieve. The use children can make of their learning depends on their approach.

Surface learning happens when the child sees a task or activity as imposed on them. In this case, they look for superficial facts to memorise so that they can do well in tests (written or whole-class questioning). They do not relate the new information to their own experiences or to previous learning, and so find it hard to recall later. They are not especially interested or motivated. They will not continue to take part in the task or activity without supervision.

Deep learning happens when the child feels an interest in the task and is personally motivated to engage with an activity. The child relates new knowledge to previous knowledge, and theoretical ideas to everyday experience.

They are able to organise and structure new learning into coherent understanding. Because the emphasis is on reflection and understanding, they are better able to remember the new learning. They are not engaged with quickly skimming through facts that can be easily tested, but with constructing a real understanding that can influence their thinking. They will continue to show an interest in the task or activity if unsupervised.

Children may be pushed into adopting surface learning strategies in order to cope with an over-demanding curriculum, interrogative questioning, or written assessment. Surface learning can get you by, in classrooms. Reassuringly, surface learning styles may become a basis for a subsequent deep learning approach.

Lev Vygotsky and learning tools

Deep learning is our aim in the classroom. One straightforward way to ensure that children work in this way is to provide them with some basic learning tools. Russian psychologist Lev Vygotsky's (1896–1934) writing tells us that spoken language is an essential tool with which children make meaning and organise thinking. Children use talk to think and learn. Their capacity to take part in deep learning depends on how well they listen, discuss, enter into dialogue and negotiation, and take part in work sharing, interpreting and judging. So it is that their understanding of the importance of their talk with others can affect how they take up chances to learn.

Teaching children how to listen and helping them to increase their repertoire of spoken language tools is a powerful way to support their engagement with their own learning, and encourage deep learning. We neglect this area of children's development – the direct teaching of speaking and listening – at our peril. Those children who have no understanding of how to talk rationally and clearly to other people are going to have to find other means to make an impression on society; for some, this may be constructive and imaginative. They may become, for example, musicians, carers or academics. However, the lack of spoken language skills can lead to a downward spiral of disaffection and disengagement with society. We may witness the tragic consequences of this in the behaviour of youngsters – and others – in our cities, towns, villages, in Internet rooms, shopping centres, parks and public spaces.

The connection between speech and thinking is evident; this is definitely not to say that all thought goes on through language. However, learning about oral language is a good introduction to some sorts of thinking that will be of value to children throughout their lives.

Spoken language tools

We can teach children to use and understand the vocabulary associated with higher order thinking. These vocabulary items can be thought of as language tools. Examples of language tools are:

- To ask questions that support one another's thinking:

    'What do you think?'

    'Why do you think that?'

    'Let's think again . . .'

- To encourage one another to elaborate or add detail:

    'Can you say a bit more?'

    'What else do we know?'

    'I can tell you about . . .'

    'Can you explain . . .'

    'I hadn't thought of that till you said it . . .'

    '[name] pointed out to me that . . .'

- To challenge one another's thinking, with respect and interest:

    'I disagree because . . .'

    'But . . .'

    'I agree but . . .'

    'You're right in my opinion . . .'

    'I believe that . . .'

    'I think . . .'

    'Another point of view is . . . .'

    'So-and-so said – and I can't see how your view fits with . . .'

- To justify what they assert:

    'My reason for saying that is . . .'

    'Because . . .'

    'I have noticed that . . .'

    'I have found out that . . .'

    'I see it differently . . .'

- To speculate:

    'If . . .'

    'What if . . .'

'Why . . .'

'Maybe we could . . .'

'I have a suggestion . . .'

- To be able to negotiate and change their mind:

    'I see what you mean . . .'

    'I am beginning to understand . . .'

    'That's a good way to look at it . . .'

    'When you put it that way . . .'

    'You have convinced me . . . .'

    'Your reason sounds right because . . .'

Development in speaking and listening is not just a matter of parroting key phrases. It requires children to gain a more profound insight into the nature of language and its crucial uses for learning.

Thinking together

This book provides an approach to teaching children how to use spoken language to reason, negotiate, think aloud with others, to solve problems and dilemmas, to find out what they want to find out so that they can learn what they are interested in learning. It draws on many years of well-established research in which the direct teaching of group talk skills has helped children to do better at reasoning, learn more effectively in curriculum areas, and become more able to think things through when working alone.

The Thinking Together team has, since 1988, conducted research in primary and secondary classrooms to look at the impact of the direct teaching of spoken language skills (Mercer and Littleton 2007). In summary, research evidence indicates that:

- Generally, children are not aware of the crucial importance of talk for thinking and learning.

- Teachers can help children to become more aware of talk for learning.

- Children benefit from the direct teaching of specific talk skills.

- This benefit is educational, in that they are able to make better use of their classroom experiences.

- The benefit is also social, in that children are better able to relate to and collaborate with one another.

Guest Speaker: Douglas Barnes, Reader in Education at the University of Leeds, 1966–1989

Learning and the role of language

To explain the importance of talk in learning, we have to consider both what the learner does, and how he or she relates and interacts with other people. We can begin with the tradition of ideas about learning called 'constructivism'. Its central contention is that each of us can only learn by making sense of what happens to us, through actively constructing a world for ourselves. Most learning does not happen suddenly: we do not one moment fail to understand something, and the next minute grasp it entirely. To take an example, compare the conception of electricity you had as a child with your understanding of it now. As a child you used the word correctly, no doubt, but you lacked the ability to analyse and explain, as well as to make links with those purposes and implications which make electricity important. Most of our systems of ideas – call them schemes, frames, models or concepts – go through a history of development in our minds, some of them changing continually throughout our lives.

One implication of this is that learning is seldom a simple matter of adding bits of information to an existing store of knowledge – though some adults have received this idea of learning from their own schooling. Most of our important learning, in school or out, is a matter of constructing models of the world, finding how far they work by using them, and then reshaping them in the light of what happens. Each new model or scheme potentially changes how we experience some aspect of the world, and therefore how we act on it. Information that finds no place in our existing schemes is quickly forgotten. That is why some pupils seem to forget so easily from one lesson to the next: the material that was presented to them made no connection with their pictures of the world.

New learning, then, depends crucially on what the learner already knows. When we are told something we can only make sense of it in terms of our existing schemes. A child who has had no experience of blowing up balloons or pumping up bicycle tyres will make much less sense of a lesson on air pressure, however clearly it is presented, than a child who has had such experience.

There are various ways of working on understanding, that is, reshaping old knowledge in the light of new ways of seeing things. The readiest way of working on understanding is often through talk, because the flexibility of speech makes it easy for us to try out new ways of arranging what we know, and easy too to change them if they seem inadequate. Of particular importance is the fact that we can talk to one another, collaborating and trying out new ways of thinking.

Not all kinds of talk are likely to contribute equally to working on understanding. It is useful to distinguish two functions of talk, according to whether the speaker's attention is primarily focused on the needs of an audience, or whether he or she is more concerned with sorting out his or her own thoughts. These two functions can be called *presentational* and *exploratory*.

Presentational talk offers a 'final draft' for display and evaluation; it is often much influenced by what the audience expects. Presentational talk frequently occurs in response to teachers' questions.

Exploratory talk is often hesitant and incomplete; it enables the speaker to try out ideas, to hear how they sound, to see what others make of them, to arrange information and ideas into different patterns. Learners are unlikely to embark on it unless they feel relatively at ease, free from the danger of being aggressively contradicted or made fun of. Exploratory talk provides an important means of working on understanding.

- The benefit is individual, in that by learning how to think aloud with others, children become better at thinking when working alone, having assimilated a good model for higher order thinking.

- Classes who learn about talk and agree a set of ground rules for exploratory talk gain more from group work.

- They are also able to tackle a range of different learning opportunities (whole-class talk, group and pair work, active learning, collaboration with children from other classes) with confidence.

- They develop productive teaching and learning relationships with adults.

- They are more likely to engage in deep learning because their own ideas, concerns and suggestions are negotiated and discussed.

Children learning in English as an additional language (EAL)

Some children can speak and listen much better in a language other than English, but are largely expected to learn in English in school. Their capacity to think in more than one language is of great value, but while they are developing an understanding of English for learning, they may find classroom conversations extremely demanding. These children can benefit from learning language structures that will help them to converse more fluently with others, including their teacher:

> EAL learners have to learn a new language while learning through the medium of that new language. This presents two main tasks in the school or setting: they need to learn English and they need to learn the content of the curriculum. To ensure that they reach their potential, learning and teaching approaches must be deployed that ensure both access to the curriculum at a cognitively appropriate level and the best opportunities for maximum language development.
>
> (DfES 2006)

This book provides activities in which spoken language is thoughtful, valued and constructive. Bilingual children with EAL can expect to speak and listen with their classmates; to have chances to reflect on and rehearse what they will say, and to hear others using language both fluently and tentatively.

About learning intentions

The activities in this book have specified learning intentions (or objectives) to share with children (Clarke 2001). Those to do with speaking and listening would usually be considered 'background' learning intentions. Teachers may rarely make these background intentions explicit but are highly likely to believe that are of utmost importance (Black *et al.* 2004). It would be good if there were explicit speaking and listening learning intentions for every classroom activity. The activities in this book should always be preceded by explaining to children the relevant learning intentions so that they understand the point and purpose of the work. Children are so often asked to be quiet in class, but really we need them to talk. It is much less likely that they will waste time and drift off task once they understand *why* we ask them to talk together.

Notes

Drama is integrated into activities in all chapters, as is ICT use. In this book 'group' means a group of two or more children usually working without adult supervision. Little special mention has been made of children with learning difficulties because this is an inclusive approach, needing no differentiation.

Abbreviation: in this book IWB stands for interactive white board.

Further reading

Daniels, H. (2001) *Vygotsky and Pedagogy.* London: Routledge.

Dawes, L., Wegerif, R. and Mercer, N. (2004) *Thinking Together: A Programme of Activities for Developing Speaking, Listening and Thinking Skills for Children Aged 8–11.* Birmingham: Questions Publishing.

CHAPTER 1

Class talk skills

Raising children's awareness of the importance of talk for learning

> Getting the knowledge from 'out there' to 'in here' is
> something for the child [. . .] to do: the art of teaching
> is knowing how to help them do it.
>
> (Douglas Barnes 1992: 79)

Conversations start, finish and punctuate the teaching day. Learning happens during talk between teachers and children. Teachers use talk for a range of purposes:

As teachers, we are aware of these purposes. But children may not know how important it is to take part in whole-class talk sessions with their teacher and classmates. They may not have realised that lesson introductions or closing plenaries are anything but pleasant and rather relaxed episodes; the educational purpose and impact of such sessions that take place might elude them. The majority of children will have well-developed oral language, but individuals may not know how to speak, listen, think and learn in the way that is expected of them in a classroom. That is, they may be unaware or confused about the basic class ground rules because these are rarely made explicit.

We can teach children the awareness, language skills and understanding that they need to take part fully in class talk, and so help them to make the most of every learning experience they are offered.

What do children think about talk in class?

It is useful to ask them. In whole-class talk sessions, any particular child might enjoy listening and talking, or may prefer to be quiet, may dream a little, or fidget, or try very hard to join in, their contribution will depend on such factors as the time of day, the subject under discussion, and who they are sitting with.

Year 5 children, asked for their ideas about classroom talk, said:

1   **We don't learn about talk in school.** Children may never have had specific lessons in which they are taught about 'talk for learning'. Or perhaps they may not have clearly understood the intentions for their learning of speaking and listening, which may not be as well defined as those in other areas.

2   **I learned to talk before I started school.** Children may believe that they learn to talk at home; that they knew how to talk when they came to school. In a way, they are right, but there are specialised types of spoken language which are of great value to them in school, and which they may still need to learn.

3   **School work is reading and writing, and not talking. You have to be quiet in class.** Children may not 'see' talk. Its influence on their minds can be hard to perceive. Talk seems to leave no evidence; there is no obvious product to show or share. It is invisible, ephemeral and seems to vanish into the air. Children may not think of it except as something they are often requested not to do.

4 **I don't think that talk is important.** Speaking and listening can seem completely unimportant because it is very low-tech, needing no special tools or equipment, not even a pencil or a book.

5 **I know how to talk now. I don't need to learn any more.** Children arriving at school are indeed usually very good at using talk for many purposes. They may not see developing speaking and listening as a set of skills and competences, and may not realise that they don't know all there is to know about it.

What can we do to help every child learn during whole-class talk?

Emeritus Professor in the Faculty of Education, University of Cambridge, Maurice Galton points out that children need help to become 'metacognitively wise' (Galton 2007). In order to use their minds effectively, they need to be taught how to do so, and what happens when they do so. Throughout Key Stage 2, children begin to understand that they can reflect on things that interest them. They can choose to keep learning. They can read for themselves and talk about what they know. They can enjoy applying their mind to problems and ideas. Children do not go through this *learning about learning* alone; it is a social process. Classrooms offer the chance to learn how to think if we can make the link between speaking, listening, thinking and learning explicit.

We teachers like the idea that children share their ideas, collaborating with others, but classrooms are high-risk places where children may find that their ideas are rejected, ridiculed or ignored. Some ideas are tenuous and easily altered; other ideas are creative, firmly held and profoundly important. Children need to know what will happen when they speak out. Galton considers the *level of risk* of activities (how much the child's thinking is exposed) in addition to *how ambiguous an outcome is possible* (whether they will gain or lose confidence). He suggests establishing a classroom atmosphere in which children and teachers feel themselves to be part of a learning community:

> In such classrooms teachers can explore with their pupils the emotional conditions of learning as well as the cognitive aspects. In such a climate it becomes possible to hold discussions about 'fear of failure' by asking the children what it feels like when I (the teacher) choose you (the pupil) to answer a question in front of the rest of the class.
>
> (Galton 2007: 92–3)

Starting points for class talk skills

An overall aim is to make a positive *change* to children's attitudes to talk in class, if you believe this to be necessary. The following sessions are designed to involve everyone, generate *dialogue* and help children reflect on what has happened. With this experience in common, children can come to whole-class sessions with prepared minds, knowing how and why to contribute, and knowing how important their contributions are to you, each other – and themselves.

What is dialogue?

Dialogue is talk in which everyone's ideas are openly shared, and discussed respectfully. Dialogue has a real impact on learning; such talk helps children to articulate their own ideas, hear new ideas, and so move on in their thinking.

CLASS TALK SKILLS ACTIVITIES

1 Talk circles

Before this session, you may have asked children, 'What do you think about talk in class?' and 'What does it feel like when I ask you a question in front of the class?'

Outline
Teacher and children take part in a dialogue to discover starting ideas; the children talk to one another in a structured way, using pictures or books as a context.

This shared opportunity is used in the plenary to help children reflect on the importance of talk, raising their awareness of their own contributions.

Skills in this session
- describing
- listening
- asking questions
- hand signal stop
- talking to a partner.

Learning intention
To know that talk skills can be learned, and that talk is used to 'get things done' together in class.

***Guest Speaker*: Rupert Wegerif, Professor of Education, University of Exeter**

More about speaking and listening for thinking

Thinking skills are often seen as the property of individuals, so how does engaging in dialogue with others influence the development of individual thinking skills? The evidence increasingly suggests that we learn to think for ourselves by first being drawn into dialogues with others. In dialogue with their parents, even in non-verbal 'peek-a-boo' games, young children learn that things can be seen in different ways from different perspectives. To learn something new, even to understand a sign as simple as a mother pointing at a teddy bear, is to be drawn into taking the perspective of another person. Once a child can take the perspective of another person, that child is ready to learn anything.

Listening to the perspective of another person in a dialogue is never simply passive. Really listening to someone else always involves generating our own answering words. So listening is already a kind of speaking. It is also true that speaking, in a dialogue at least, is already a kind of listening because it is necessary to take on the perspective of those we are talking with in order to shape our words to speak to them. Most important, learning is creative in that it requires a leap to see things in a new way. It is hard to understand how this is possible until we see people getting 'carried away' and 'drawn out of themselves' when talking together with others. In dialogues people often find themselves saying things that, before the dialogue, they did not yet know that they knew.

By teaching children to engage more effectively in dialogues with others, we are teaching the most general thinking and learning skill of all. So-called 'higher order thinking skills', such as creativity, reasoning, evaluating and reflective self-monitoring, appear to originate in and be practised in the context of dialogue. All such thinking skills are the fruits of dialogue, and the best way to teach engagement in dialogue and more effective dialogue in the primary curriculum is through a focus on the quality of speaking and listening.

Resources

Use **1.1 City wildlife** below *or* pictures from magazines/reading books/pictures of people.

1.1 City wildlife

Introduction

Ask the children to think about talk, using starter questions which invite thoughtful responses:

- How did you learn to talk?

- Do you think you are still learning to talk, or can you do it as well as possible, now?

- Who do you like talking to? Why?

– What jobs do you get done through talk – at home?

– What things do you get done through talk – at school? – in class? – at play?

– Do you think it is hard to listen in class? Why?

– Do you think it is important to talk to classmates during group work? Why?

Group work

Explain the learning intentions, and point out that children are expected to work with everyone else in the class. Decide on a hand signal (e.g. hand up with palm forward) which means 'please stop talking immediately'. Practise use of the signal and ask the children to decide why this is necessary in a classroom.

Choose two children to model the group work. Provide one of them with a picture. Explain that the activity involves *using talk* to do two things:

a) the child with picture will describe it to the other child (ensure that all know what 'describe' really means);

b) the child with no picture listens and asks questions.

Allow 30 seconds to do this – longer if you feel it is appropriate.

Divide the class into two equal sized groups. Ask the children to form two circles, one inside the other. Provide the children in the outer circle with a picture. Ask the children to rotate so that the inner circle moves clockwise, the outer anticlockwise. Choose when to stop. Ask children to speak/listen as modelled. Remind the children to think about the volume needed for talking to a nearby partner.

Stop, using your hand signal; ask children to give the picture/book to their partner.

Rotate again. Stop; this time the child in the inner circle describes while the outer child listens and questions.

Plenary

Ask a confident child to recall the description they heard. Ask the partner named to say how they could tell they were being listened to. Ask this child to nominate another to talk about their experience. Carry on this chain so that children are contributing without raising hands. Finally, ask the whole class:

– Who was good to talk to?

– Who was a good listener?

– What was interesting?

– Why is it important to listen to other people in our class?

2 Collections

Learning intention
To share ideas through talk with others.

Resources

- *Old Hat, New Hat* by Stan and Jan Berenstain.

- Collection of hats: baseball hats, woolly hats, hard hat, wizard hat, sun hat, party hats, etc. One hat per child is ideal but one between two is plenty.

- *Or* other collection – children's shoes, PE balls, egg cups, marbles, teachers' mugs, cushions, chairs, leaves – whatever you can readily collect.

- One copy per child of **1.2 Describing hats** (re-purpose for other collections).

Introduction
Tell the children that they are all going to help each other think of some good describing words, or adjectives. Start by thinking about *collections* of things. Ask them to talk to one another about anything that they, or their family, collect. Show the hats (or other collection) and explain that they are all slightly different. If we had to describe them to someone else, or had to write an advert to sell a hat, we would need some good describing words or adjectives.

- Read *Old Hat, New Hat*.

- Distribute the hat collection, stressing that the hats are to look at, not to wear (hygiene!).

- Ask groups to talk together to think of some good words – at least one or two – to describe their hat (stripy, starry, flowery, squashy, red, cardboard, ridiculous, sensible, etc.), then to choose their favourite word.

- Read the beginning of *Old Hat, New Hat* again. When the customer starts looking at new hats, each group in turn stands up and shows their hat and joins in with 'Too . . . [pink, spotty, big; etc.]'. Finish the story.

Group work
Tell the children that they will be sharing their describing words with anyone in the class who asks them to. Provide **1.2 Describing hats.** Ask the children to draw and describe their own hat in the first box, then choose any other child in the class, move to sit near them, draw and describe their hat by asking the hat keeper for their words.

After drawing eight hats, the children can design and describe some imaginary hats.

Stress the learning intention of sharing ideas.

1.2 Describing hats

My name is

I worked with

My hat	_____ 's hat
My adjectives	adjectives
_____ 's hat	_____ 's hat
adjectives	adjectives
_____ 's hat	_____ 's hat
adjectives	adjectives
_____ 's hat	_____ 's hat
adjectives	adjectives

My hat designs: rain hat   sun hat   party hat – with adjectives

Plenary

Ask children to walk carefully around the tables, looking at the work and noticing effective drawing or interesting words. Use post-it notes to leave a positive comment. Review 'collections' work. Ask children to say who helped them by talking to them, by suggesting ideas, helping with drawing, sharing hats, and so on. Ask children to decide if the learning intention of sharing through talk was achieved.

3 Where does talk go?

Outline

Talk is made to seem more concrete. Children learn that talk does not vanish but has an impact on other people's minds.

Skills in this session

* courteous requests
* active listening
* recall
* awareness of learning.

Learning intention

To understand that talk affects thinking.

Resources

Use **1.3 Jake's first week** and **1.4 Favourites record** (one per child).

Introduction

Ask children what happens to spoken language; where does it all go?

Explain that you are going to give an example of spoken language. Read *Jake's First Week*. Ask where the spoken words have gone. They may say that the words are in their minds; they may not. Ask children to articulate their ideas about *memory*. What can they recall about the story? Does everyone's memory of it match? Bring out this idea of spoken words for sharing stories, ideas and information, and for joint recall.

Ask for anecdotes: what happened yesterday evening; a funny story about a pet; an account of a playground game. After this distraction, ask children to recall key ideas from the story. Point out that talk hasn't vanished; we retain it in our memory.

Group work

You may wish to model this activity before everyone starts.

Provide every child with **1.4 Favourites record** and ask them to write their name.

Explain that they are going to work with everyone else in the class. They are going to ask their classmates questions, and thank them for their contributions. They are going to remember what they are told, but also keep a record on paper.

Starting with the person next to them, the child asks:

'Please could you choose one row and say what is your favourite?'

Example: The row chosen is *holiday*, favourite holiday *seaside*. The partner writes their name/initials in the first space and draws a small picture or logo to represent their favourite – perhaps sun or an ice cream cone – then returns the record. Children thank each other for contributions. In this way children move around the entire classroom, collecting information from all other children in the class. Early finishers can ask for favourites in a second category from children they have already 'interviewed'.

Plenary

Collect the **Favourites records**. Ask children to recall examples of who liked what. Ask them to say who was helpful and drew useful pictures. What have they learned about one another? Where did the talk go? Point out that the record cards might help us remember for longer, but that our minds 'soak up' talk and store it.

Ask further questions about **Jake's first week** (or other previous learning) as an example of memory.

For example:

- What was the teacher called?

- What did Jake do that worried his classmates?

- Who did Jake sit next to on Friday?

- When we talked about the story, who said what about it?

- What do you remember thinking about what they said?

Ask the children to reflect. Who seems to have a good memory? How can you help yourself remember things better? Stress the importance of listening. Bring out the idea that talking about things with others is a way of thinking aloud, and that we can help one another recall things by talking. Discuss achievement of the learning intentions.

Favourites records can be displayed and used for later discussion about memory.

1.3 Jake's first week

On Monday, Jake arrived in Miss Fisher's class. He sat next to Tyler. As soon as they started work, he snapped Tyler's pencil in half. This was not a good start.

On Tuesday, Jake was sitting next to Ellie. In literacy, he took her rubber and broke it in two. On Wednesday, Jake was at a different table, sitting next to Niall. In Science, he picked up Niall's ruler. He held it in both hands and bent it backwards and forwards. Suddenly it broke with a loud snap.

On Thursday, Jake was in Dami's group for PE. In the middle of the game, he took a great big bite out of the yellow sponge ball. It was ruined. Jake didn't seem to mind.

On Friday, it was numeracy, and the class were drawing triangles. Miss Fisher asked Jake to sit next to Freddie. Freddie smiled at Jake.

Jake snapped Freddie's pencil in two.

'Oh good,' said Freddie. 'Two little pencils. We can have one each.'

Jake snapped Freddie's rubber in two.

'A piece for you and a piece for me,' said Freddie.

Jake picked up the ruler.

'It's such a nice long ruler,' said Freddie. 'You can borrow it.' And he smiled again.

Jake didn't snap it. He used it to draw a long line with his little pencil.

'You're good at that,' said Freddie. 'Can you draw a line for me?'

Jake drew a line for Freddie. Miss Fisher came to talk to them.

'What are you two doing?' she said.

'Nothing,' said Jake.

'Sharing,' said Freddie.

'Drawing big triangles!' said Miss Fisher. 'Well done.'

1.4 Favourites record

my name is:

Holiday				
Day of the week				
Sport				
Toy				
Drink				

4 Playing out

Outline

Children practise asking one another the key language tool 'What do you think?' and reflect on the outcomes of both listening, and explaining their ideas, for their own learning.

Skills in this session
* articulating thoughts
* listening and responding.

Learning intention

To use the questions, 'What do you think?' and 'Why?'.

Resources

– Shoe box with toy, taped or locked in.

– Selection of tools – key, spanner, screwdriver, tape measure, torch, pencil, wooden spoon, scissors.

Introduction

Ask the children to guess what is in the box. Ask for suggestions of which tools we could use to open the box without damaging it. Open the box and let one child only see what is inside.

Point out that this child knows an awful lot of things – their mind is like the closed box. We need to find out what they know about what's in the box; how can we do this? Can we use any of the tools without damaging the child? What 'tool' can we use to find out what is in the child's mind? Lead the children to suggest 'asking questions'. Encourage questions which will help the child to give clues about the secret toy.

Go on to encourage the children to use questions to find out what else this child (or another child) has in their mind. For example, what is your favourite colour? When is your birthday? Do you have a pet? What do you think about . . . (book, story, TV programme, school issues?).

Explain that questions are talk tools that do the useful job of finding out what people know or understand. Remind the class that they have successfully used questions before. Now they are going to learn to use a special question – a special talk tool. Use the analogy of scissors: good questions are like sharp scissors – they really work. The special question, 'What do you think?' can really help to find out what is in someone's mind.

Model question-and-answer sequences with the volunteer child.

'Some people think weekends should be three days long. What do you think?'

Point out that the child may give a reason ('I think . . . *because* . . .'). If they don't, however, a good way to encourage them to give a reason is to ask 'Why?'.

For example, when a reason is given:

'I think two days is long enough *because* I only see my friends in school.'

When a reason is not given:

'I think it would be good to have three days.'
'Why?'
'*Because* I could go swimming at weekends if I had an extra day.'

Group work

Use **1.5 Talking Points: playing out**. Read the information, then discuss ideas using the 'Talking Points'. These are statements for reflection and discussion which can help children to articulate their ideas, listen to others, and rehearse sensible ways to agree and disagree with a range of opinions.

Discuss with children the ways they can share ideas, challenge one another with respect, listen and encourage one another, and find out what everyone thinks.

Display 'Information about Talking Points'.

Information about Talking Points

- Talk and think together to share everyone's ideas and opinions.

- Remember to ask other people 'What do you think?'

- Ask 'Why?' to find out their reasons.

- Use 'I agree, because . . .'

- *Or* 'I disagree, because . . .' to challenge others with respect.

- Listen and think what else you can add to the discussion.

1.5 Talking Points: playing out information

A surprising number of children playing outside are told off by adults because they are making a noise, or creating a disturbance. The Children's Society says that children are 'having their development stifled' by grumpy adults. The charity talked to 2,600 children aged 7 to 16 and found that two-thirds of them liked to play outside daily, mostly to meet friends.

- An eight-year-old girl was stopped from cycling down her street because a neighbour complained the wheels squeaked.

- An angry neighbour burst a ball belonging to a three-year-old boy when it bounced over her hedge.

- Some 80 per cent of children had been told off for playing outdoors and 50 per cent had been shouted at.

- Of children aged 7 to 11, about half had been told off by parents and 15 per cent by neighbours.

- One in three children said that being told off stopped them playing out.

- For some reason, 11-year-olds were more likely to be told off than any other age group!

- Children are often banned from playing on grass or are told that they can not use skateboards or bikes, or have basketball or netball hoops on walls.

Parents organise structured play for their children after school, such as music, dance, swimming, football, drama classes and tennis lessons. Children have very little chance for unstructured or free play – and even less chance of playing outdoors. An American study found that the average American child spends only 25 minutes a week involved in unstructured play outdoors – that's only four minutes a day playing outside!

Start your discussion by taking it in turns to share your experience of playing outside. Listen while others tell you about themselves for a few minutes.

- Are you allowed to play out?

- What rules are there?

- Who do you play with?

- What do you like to do?

- If you are not allowed out, do you know why not?

- Would you like to play out?

- What do you think would be good about it?

1.5 Talking Points: playing out discussion

What does your group think?
Do you agree, or disagree, and what
are your reasons?

1　Playing outdoors is healthy exercise for children.

2　Meeting people outdoors helps children to get on well with one another.

3　You can hurt yourself by playing on climbing frames and swings, so it is better not to.

4　Adults buy homes and own parks, so they should say if children are allowed to play around them or not.

5　There are lots of things to do at home such as computer games and watching TV, so children should stay at home.

6　Playing outside is a waste of time. Structured play teaches you more.

7　Outdoor places should have lots of plants, animals, trees, water, sand, mud.

8　Children should help design play spaces near their homes.

9　We do not have very much free time to play.

10　Playing outside can make you feel fit, strong and healthy.

11　Nature is boring and playing out is dull. It's more fun to stay in.

12　It is dangerous to play out.

Design a survey

With your group, make up five questions that you could ask children to find out their experience of playing out.

Think of questions that would help children give facts about whether they play out; say what they like and don't like, and help them to tell you their opinions.

Plenary

Ask for ideas and opinions about 'playing out'.

Discuss the learning intention in the light of group work and ask the following questions. Who helped you learn? Who asked you what you thought? Was the discussion effective? Why? If there have been problems, how can things be changed before next time? Can you say how talk helped your thinking or expanded your ideas?

Extension

Ask children to role play the advantages and disadvantages of playing out; use the children's questions to conduct a survey of other children in the school; relate the discussion to local play areas and the school playground; use the information to talk to governors and parents about the issues as the children see them.

5 How important is talk?

Outline
The link between talking and thinking is made evident.

Skills in this session
- collaboration
- joint creativity
- active listening.

Learning intention
To know that talking is a way of thinking aloud.

Resources
Use **1.6 Griffey's walk** (one per child).

Introduction
Ask children to share their ideas about *talk*; discuss these questions with the person next to them, before inviting individuals to say what they think to the whole class:

- Who is good at talking, and why do you think so?

- Who do you like to talk to, at school and at home, and why?

- When do you like to be quiet?

Explain that talk is a way of thinking aloud. Unless we talk to people they are likely to guess what we are thinking – and they may be wrong, in ways that can make life difficult. Also, even when we do talk, sometimes it's hard to say exactly what we mean, and misunderstandings do arise.

Explain the activity: to talk and think together to complete a story. Everyone will have useful ideas, and it's important that these are shared in a friendly way. The work in this session is the discussion; what others say should be valued by listening, challenging or agreeing, and showing respect for ideas. The group do not have to agree what to write; each child will make their own copy of the story later. The purpose of collaboration is to stimulate imagination and generate a range of ideas through talk.

Group work

Provide every child with a copy of **1.6 Griffey's walk**. Describe the tasks to be done:

1   Talk and think together to say what is happening in each scene.

2   Talk and think together to decide what Griffey and the people are saying in each box, and write speech bubbles. Each child completes an individual copy, making sure they help one another to finish, using their own or shared ideas.

3   Talk and think together to decide who else Griffey can ask to take her for a walk. What is the person doing? Draw a picture, caption and speech bubble to show your ideas.

4   On the back of the sheet, draw a cartoon box to finish the story. This could be what happens when Griffey returns home, or perhaps what happens if Griffey continues on her journey with the aliens.

5   Talk together to decide on a new title for the finished cartoon.

Plenary

Ask children to leave their cartoons at their places. Provide everyone with post-it notes. Ask everyone to move around the room, looking at each other's work, and adding a post-it with a positive comment. Stress that children are looking for what others have done well – art work, speech bubbles, ideas, story ending.

With children back in their places, allow time to look at comments. Ask for feedback about the group work. Was it easy to share ideas? Was anyone particularly helpful? Did talking to others help the children to think about their stories and do their best?

Point out that talking is thinking aloud, and that thinking aloud together is a way of collaborating – that is, getting on well with others. Stress that the

1.6 Griffey's walk

Griffey asked Kyra to take her for a walk.

Griffey asked Dad to take her for a walk.

Next, Griffey tried Arran.

Poppy wanted to help but she couldn't walk yet.

Griffey thought the aliens said "Take me to your lead..."

Griffey got her lead and went with the aliens.

Griffey had a moon walk.

learning is in the talk, and that people often do better if they have chance to talk to other people about what they are doing.

Discuss problems. Was it easy to stay on task? Did anyone fall out or argue in a way that was not helpful? What can others suggest to get round any problems next time there is group work? Keep a record of suggestions, and check that there is chance to put them into practice and evaluate them.

Do the class feel that the learning intentions have been achieved?

Extension

a) The cartoons can be changed into written stories, or displayed, or acted out.

b) Ask the children to talk and think together to draw a similar cartoon in their groups.

Put into practice ideas for collaboration suggested in the whole-class talk.

The plenary can be used to check if these strategies were effective, and if not, decide what to do about it.

Children can make up their own stories, or use the following outline as a basis:

Merla and the mouse

Merla is a small cat. She is hungry. She asks people to feed her – the cartoon shows her asking people one after another; everyone refuses to give her some food.

Merla is sitting looking at her box of cat biscuits when she notices a mouse behind the box. Merla is just about to pounce when the mouse starts gnawing the corner of the box.

Biscuits fall out and Merla shares them with the mouse.

Summary

Children can learn how to join in with class talk. They can reflect on and discuss the point and purpose of whole-class talk, gaining the confidence to take part. They can become more aware of the importance of active listening and respect for others.

They can use questions and answers, particularly the question 'What do you think?'

Talking Points are one way to structure and stimulate group talk. Children also benefit from awareness of the importance of collaboration and providing positive feedback for others. By considering their own role in class talk for thinking and learning, children have the opportunity to understand how readily they can help one another to learn.

Further reading

Barnes, D. (1992) *From Communication to Curriculum.* Portsmouth, NH: Boynton/Cook.

Galton, M. (2007) *Learning and Teaching in the Primary Classroom.* London: Sage.

CHAPTER 2

Talking Points

A strategy for encouraging dialogue between children and in whole-class sessions

Teachers should deliberately encourage and support their pupils in developing an open and hypothetical style of learning.

(Barnes 1992: 9)

The important thing is not to stop questioning.

(Albert Einstein)

About Talking Points

Talking Points offer a strategy for stimulating speaking, listening, thinking and learning. Talking Points are basically a list of thoughts – statements which may be factually accurate, contentious or downright wrong. They provide a focus for speaking and listening, and a chance to find out what others think. They can be thought-provoking, interesting, irritating, amusing, smart, simple, brief or wordy. Talking Points are easy to make up, read and understand, but offer ways into thinking more deeply about the subject under discussion. They enable everyone to say what is in their minds, so that others can decide whether they agree or disagree.

So that there is plenty to talk about, there are always rather a lot of Talking Points. Some groups become so involved that they never get to the end of the list – and this is good. High quality talk always takes time. Early finishers are offered a joint, creative task at the end of the list, which draws on their discussion and extends thinking. You may want to ask children to concentrate on particular points.

Before the discussion using Talking Points

Children work in groups. One child should be able to read the Talking Points on behalf of the others; if all are fluent readers, the group can take turns. They should be aware that speaking and listening, not reading, is the focus. It is everyone's responsibility to make sure that everyone else is asked for their opinion. Everyone must think about what is said, checking whether they agree or disagree, or can add further information. No time limit is set. Each group must monitor its own members, making sure that no one feels left out, and that challenges are sensible and respectful of others. In particular, everyone is asked to give reasons for what they say. The question 'Why?' should occur constantly.

Groups should be aware that they will be asked to contribute to a whole-class plenary about two things: (a) the content of the Talking Points, and (b) how well the group talked and worked together. They should be able to identify and remember who asked a helpful question, changed their mind, encouraged someone else to talk, provided interesting ideas or information, and so on.

Children should know that they will only be asked for positive comments on one another's speaking and listening. Their explanation of difficulties should be reported objectively without apportioning blame; otherwise, resentments may be taken out of the classroom. Children can learn to use language tools such as:

'My group found it hard to agree about . . .'

'We fell out about . . .'

'Our problem was . . .'

These help to indicate that it is the entire group that has to reflect and adjust, not just one problem child. Difficulties can be discussed and evaluated as a basis for developing new talk strategies to try out.

Make sure everyone understands the hand signal for 'stop talking please', and knows why it is important to co-operate in this way. Also, make sure that children know that they should be talking to someone very nearby at a sensible volume.

During the discussion

Group discussion is a terrific opportunity to find out what children really think. It's good to be drawn into a discussion when you know that a word or a question will set off new and helpful trains of thought. It is often a good idea to chip in and move a group's thinking along – but a light touch is required. Similarly, well-prepared teaching assistants can very well support, encourage and promote group talk.

Sometimes, groups will take the easy option and give surface answers, whizzing through the list of Talking Points with little engagement. The teacher can re-start the group on a particular point, asking for their ideas or reasons, or can ask the group to disband and become observant listeners to other groups, learning a more productive model of discussion for next time.

Talking Points plenary discussions

Take a Talking Point which has raised uncertainty or interest, and ask one group to explain their thinking about it. Draw on what you have heard during group work, and ask particular children to repeat what they said. Everyone should have something to say, so 'hands up' isn't necessary. Use the *nomination* strategy, which is to ask a child who has spoken to the whole class to choose who contributes next. Contributions may need summing up and rephrasing for clarity, but the discussion can proceed with children choosing who they think they want to hear from. Ask the class to choose girl-boy-girl and so on if you think necessary. This part of the lesson is a chance to give positive feedback on interesting ideas and clear thinking and reasoning.

Ask children if they heard the question 'What do you think?'. Ask if everyone always agreed with what they heard, or whether they had different ideas, and if so, how were they negotiated. Ask for examples of good listening, and interesting ideas. Ask if the children enjoyed talking together. Can they think of other times when the phrase 'What do you think?' might be useful?

There is rarely time in class to deal with all the issues raised by all the groups for each Talking Point. Talking Points discussions often have an unfinished feel about them. There is benefit from having in mind questions that remain unresolved, or ideas raised that have created uncertainty. Individual learning can start from the friction of such 'wonderings', especially if children are encouraged to take their musings and queries away to share them with others.

Ask groups to provide information about how well they worked together. Children can give examples of good questions, changes of mind, asking for contributions, and so on, and you can show the child who has done these things how much you and the class value their contribution to the learning of others.

Groups who have had problems can be asked to suggest what they can do about changing things. Other groups can be asked to suggest their ideas to help.

Written work can be based on the children's discussion.

Guest Speaker: Claire Sams, Associate Lecturer, Open University and Teacher/Researcher

The role of the teacher in teaching speaking and listening

The role of the teacher in developing the quality of children's speaking and listening is crucial. Often children are asked to discuss their ideas or to work together in groups, but it soon becomes clear that many don't know what is really being asked of them. Some are happy to talk, but don't consider other people's views. Others find it hard to join in. But when a teacher makes explicit the kind of talk that is useful, the effect on children's ability to talk and think about things together is dramatic. Children who had previously been reluctant to collaborate find a voice; all ideas are carefully considered.

One of the most important things teachers do is to model the kind of speaking and listening we want children to use. This doesn't involve a huge amount of planning or preparation, but a shift in awareness about how we engage in dialogue in all parts of the lesson. Rather than doing the vast majority of talking and expecting children to listen quietly or answer questions individually, teachers can engage children in a more balanced dialogue. We can discuss with the class the kinds of phrases that help everyone to collaborate effectively when working together in groups. This doesn't take long but creates a sense of shared purpose and understanding, and helps children to draw on previous learning.

Another important aspect of the teacher's role is the way that we intervene in group talk. This can either be a great opportunity for assessing and furthering effective dialogue, or can stop it in its tracks. One of the most effective examples I came across was when a teacher joined a group discussing various choices. As she listened to the talk, she became aware that one of the children was trying to make a point but others were not responding to her ideas as she wasn't explaining them clearly. First, the teacher asked the others to give their opinions. Then she asked the child what she thought and why. Through listening to the group talk, the child was able to explain her point of view and go on to persuade the rest of the group to reconsider.

As a teacher, I found that learning how to enable children to think together created a richer and more interactive learning environment for all. This is an inclusive approach. Children of all abilities are able to contribute effectively to dialogue, once they have been taught how to use exploratory talk. Those who may otherwise find it hard to participate are not only able to do so, but can influence the outcome of a discussion. I have seen a child explain a strategy for solving a problem to other more able children, thus developing the understanding of all the children in the group, because they had been taught how to use speaking and listening effectively by their teacher while the 'more able' children had not.

Teaching speaking and listening skills is important to children; they report that they like this approach and recognise its value for learning:

> We normally say '*What do you think?*' instead of leaving someone
> out . . . [I'm not] afraid to challenge someone with their answer –
> I don't just sit there and say '*All right – pick that one I don't care*'.
> It makes us feel more confident if we're in a group.

2.1 Talking Points example: Light and shadow

Talk together to decide if these are true or false, or are you unsure?

1 We can see shadows every day.

2 Shadows are the same shape as the thing they are next to.

3 Shadows are biggest in the middle of the day.

4 A shadow is made of black dust.

5 A shadow cannot change its shape.

6 Shadows get light darker in the day and lighter in the evening.

7 You can get coloured shadows.

8 Shadows stick to our feet.

9 The sun gives us light every day.

10 The moon changes shape because of its own shadow.

11 Light can be made from electricity.

12 Light can be different colours.

13 White light is made up of a mixture of different coloured light.

Talk about and do the following individually, helping each other

• We can draw a light bulb, label all the parts, write what materials all the parts are made from, and say *why* each part is made of that material.

• We can draw a rainbow with the colours in the right order.

• We can draw a person with a big hat, long legs, and a shadow.

We can make up two Talking Points about light and shadows.

2.2 Talking Points example: The peacock butterfly

The peacock butterfly can be seen in summer feeding on thistles, marjoram or buddleia. The peacock butterfly looks almost black when its wings are closed. It is camouflaged to protect it from birds. Its open wings are a rich red with vividly coloured spots which look like eyes, in the same way that the markings on a peacock's tail look like eyes.

If a bird comes too near, the peacock butterfly will open and close its wings rapidly to flash its 'eyes' and startle the bird. Peacock butterflies seen in March have hibernated over winter. The butterflies feed on the sugar (nectar) made by flowers. They cannot grow or repair their wings if they get damaged.

Peacock butterflies mate and lay eggs. They lay their eggs on the underside of nettle leaves, because nettle leaves are the only thing that their caterpillars can eat. The caterpillars live all together in a web of silk. When they have eaten and grown, they separate and find a leaf where they can hide. Then they form a pupa or chrysalis. Inside the pupa, they change how their body is organised. In summer, the pupa splits and the butterfly emerges to dry its wings. It flies away to find food and to find others like itself.

In Britain, butterflies are disappearing faster than any other wild creature. One hundred years ago, there were a hundred times as many butterflies as there are now.

Talking Points: What does your group think?

1 Nettles are essential to peacock butterflies.

2 We need butterflies. They show us how healthy our environment is.

3 Other butterflies also use camouflage to protect themselves.

4 Butterflies grow bigger as the summer goes on.

5 Both butterflies and moths can spin silk – so can spiders.

6 We have seen a peacock butterfly and can name other sorts.

7 Butterflies are killed by the cold in winter.

8 Butterflies have cold blood and need the sun to warm up.

9 We can think of a list of other creatures that hibernate.

10 Nettles are dangerous to people, so we should cut them all down.

Talk about and do individually, helping each other

• We can draw a life-cycle of a peacock butterfly.

• We can draw a food chain with a butterfly, a blackbird and a cat.

• We can draw a butterfly, label all the parts of its body and say why it is an insect.

Do-it-yourself Talking Points

1 Think of the topics or concepts that you are, or will be, teaching. Would there be merit in some exchange of ideas; are there puzzling facts or possible misconceptions that need to be aired and examined?

2 Decide whether you want the children to have a discussion at the start of the session or topic, in the middle, or at the end. Each has advantages – at the start, to take a sounding of current understanding; during group work, to learn from and with one another; at the end, to evaluate learning and share newly conceived thoughts.

3 Find a resource – poem, story, picture or topic (such as 'magnetism' or 'the Vikings').

4 Use the resource to help you to generate around ten ideas that will get the children talking. It helps to think of the statements as having an answer – 'true, false or unsure' – that is, as statements that can be rationally considered. Talking Points puts the children in the position of having to justify their ideas and articulate their thinking. They are not questions.

5 Express your Talking Points simply and concisely.

6 Think of an extension activity; this will involve the group using their ideas to create something or do further work together. This enables those who rush their discussion (a stage on the way to learning how to think aloud with others) to be productively occupied while others talk.

7 Number the list for easy reference in discussion.

8 Prepare the children for their Talking Points session by careful grouping, reminders about talk as work, volume of talk, and the importance of thoughtful contributions.

Children's own Talking Points

Creating questions and answers stimulates higher order thinking – that is, reflection, analysis and evaluation. To generate and phrase a question, a child has to look at or experience something, match this against what they already know or understand, and reflect on where their areas of uncertainty are. It can be hard to think of what it is that you *don't* know and to put it into words. Working through this process helps children to develop their capacity to question. Once they can create questions using concrete experiences, they can begin to question and reflect on more abstract ideas. Such reflection helps children to consider their own assumptions and to check that they have thought of all relevant information. Through this process, they are learning to reason, to understand the workings of their own mind, and to be accountable to themselves and others. These are attributes that will see them in good stead throughout their lives.

Provide the class with a stimulus that relates to your topic – for example, a historical artefact, a model, toy or picture of an animal or plant, a poem, a story, a drawing or cartoon. Ask the children to talk together in their groups to decide on five things that they know about this and five they don't know. Ask the group to write five questions which they would like to ask the rest of the class, each on a separate post-it note. They can be genuine questions or ones that the group can already answer.

Now ask the class to reflect on and answer questions from other groups.

This can be organised differently to suit your class:

a) Ask children to leave their seats and walk around the tables with a partner, reading questions and writing their answers on another post-it. More than one group can add answers to any question, building up a set of information.

b) Ask groups to swap questions. Alternatively, leave questions where they are and ask groups to swap tables.

c) Provide one child from each group with a sheet of A4 paper. Ask this child to collect three or four post-its from around the room on their sheet, and return to their group to discuss and make a note of answers.

Next, ask each group to talk about one of their questions and the sorts of answers that their classmates have offered. Ask the class what they have learned and who has helped them to learn. Bring out points about the ways questions are phrased, the difference between open and closed questions, and the importance of questioning own knowledge to check for understanding and accuracy. Collect up the questions and their answers. Using these as a resource, re-phrase them as Talking Points for use in your next session, as in the example below.

Example: Looking at woodlice

A class of Year 3 children looked at woodlice in a plastic aquarium and on a brief film on the IWB. These are some of their questions and answers:

– What does it eat?	– Plants and vegetables.
– Do they have babies?	– Yes, you can get little woodlice and eggs.
– Does it have a shell?	– No not like a snail.
– How many legs does it have?	– Fourteen.
– How fast can it move?	– Some faster than others, all pretty slow.

These answers were then phrased by the teacher as Talking Points and became a talk-based starter activity for the next session.

Talking Points: The life of woodlice

With your group think together to decide if these are true, false, or are you unsure?

1   Woodlice are herbivores – they only eat plants.

2   Woodlice have babies; they do not lay eggs.

3   Woodlice have a hard outside but it is not a shell.

4   Woodlice have more legs than a spider.

5   Woodlice move at different speeds.

Summary

Talking Points offer a range of statements for reflection and discussion. Children think together about a particular topic, offering a range of points of view, ideas and information. Discussion enables children to find out what others think, know or believe, and to offer their own ideas for exploration in a non-threatening context. After discussion and sharing of ideas, questions arising can be investigated or researched. Sharing ideas through Talking Points means that those who find it hard to articulate their thoughts are helped to see ways to do so as they listen to others. Encouraging responses to tentative ideas increases children's confidence to take part in classroom talk.

Further reading

Grugeon, E., Hubbard, L., Smith, C. and Dawes, L. (1998) *Teaching Speaking and Listening in the Primary School.* London: David Fulton Press.

CHAPTER 3

Listening

Helping children to understand how and why they should become active listeners

> I wash my hands of those who imagine chattering to be
> knowledge, silence to be ignorance . . .
>
> (Kahlil Gibran)

Why listen?

Children learn to speak by listening to what is said to them and creatively putting things into words themselves. By the time they reach Key Stage 2, the vast majority of children have functional language, and can speak and listen in at least one language.

Listening is key to learning in classrooms, and yet how often do we say of a child – or a whole class – *they just don't listen!* Why don't they? Is it because they can't, and if not, why not? Are they deliberately or inadvertently choosing not to? Why would they do that? What are they thinking about instead? Perhaps we could ask them sometimes. It is crucial to recognise that when we note that in class, children *just aren't listening!* – the reasons *why not* may be a complete lack of interest in the lesson, or lack of understanding needed to make sense of what is going on. These are perennial classroom problems that teachers spend hours trying to remedy by creative planning, careful choice of resources and personalised learning programmes. Having said this – that children won't listen if they don't want to – we can also say that every child benefits from lessons in listening. Generally, when children listen in class, they learn. When they don't listen, they may lose the chance to learn and may stop others learning too. How can we help children to listen in class? It is not an easy thing to do. As much as anything, we need their help.

Listening and speaking

Developing physically depends on exercise; developing thinking depends on using spoken language. That is not to say that we cannot think without language. We can enjoy music, a sunset or a hug without ever really putting our thoughts into words. Words, however, allow us to make meaning from what we feel, to communicate our thoughts and ideas, and to organise our thinking. Listening and putting what has been heard into their own words is fundamental to children's thinking and learning.

Informal learning of spoken language – or languages, if we are lucky – continues throughout our lives. But teachers have a particular responsibility to foster and develop speaking and listening skills. Few children will achieve their true academic or intellectual potential unless they learn how to negotiate their ideas with other people through talk. The child's ability to read, write, be numerate, learn in all curriculum areas, and to be social and independent, all rest on oral language development. This is not to say that home learning of talk is unimportant; indeed, it is just the opposite. However, what the school adds to the child's understanding of talk might make a crucial difference to their ability to get the best from the formal education they are offered.

Causes of hearing loss or listening problems

It is necessary for teachers to know how the ears and brain work together to turn sound into meaning. For some children, this process does not work as well as it might. Physical causes for loss of hearing and inattention in terms of listening include problems with outer, middle or inner ear, or with the brainstem or cerebral cortex. To understand spoken words, children must be able to distinguish specific vowel and consonant sounds – e.g. cat and bat; cat and calf; want and wanted – so that they can understand. They must respond to pitch, loudness and rhythm, and understand the context of what they hear. Listening is also influenced by the room's acoustics, competition from other senses, motivation and emotional state. Sometimes a child may arrive in class so distressed or excited that their mind cannot settle to listening. Such things as a family argument or the arrival of a new baby; a birthday or the death of a pet, are truly important and necessarily affect the child's capacity to attend. Memory is also important, perhaps especially important for learners with EAL, who have to listen very carefully to follow the conversation (DfES; Inclusion).

Children who are listening well:

- look at the person who is talking;

- keep eye contact, nod, look interested;

- keep relatively still and calm;

- ask interested questions or make a relevant comment or contribution;

- are able to recall what was said and explain it.

The state of a child's mind and their emotional condition can often be gauged from how they respond or behave when asked to listen. Children ask for help by not listening.

A common problem for the teacher is how to involve thirty children in listening and thinking while only one of them speaks at a time. We can use talk partners, talk buddies, or pair and share arrangements to encourage children to talk to one another. We can make sure that children know how and why to listen when working with the whole class.

Stop!

Classrooms always need a reliable 'stop' signal that cuts through talk without having to use a raised voice. The signal can be carefully explained and used consistently. Those who respond immediately are given positive feedback. You can take a moment or two to walk around your groups while they are talking, telling each group that time is nearly up and reminding them to get ready for the stop signal.

Stop signals

Some stop signals are:

- a hand signal – hand up, palm forward;

- a rhythmic clapping signal, started by the teacher or a chosen child;

- a small metal bowl and a brass tapper;

- a gong;

- a particular song on the CD player (your choice, or child of the week's choice);

- a swanee whistle (as in *The Clangers*);

- light signal – room lights switched off for a moment then on again;

- light signal 2 – powerful torch with red filter shone in the corners of the room in turn;

- IWB switched to a particular picture or scrolling message.

Guest Speaker: **Linda Bartlett, Team Leader for the Ethnic Minority Achievement Support Service (EMASS), Milton Keynes Learning Directorate**

Developing speaking and listening: children with English as an Additional Language (EAL)

Children who are learning EAL are already proficient in speaking and listening in one or more other languages, dependent upon age and experience. Our aim is to facilitate transfer of these skills, while at the same time supporting the development of further skills in both English and first language. An EAL child can be placed along the continuum from complete beginner to advanced learner in English. Speaking and listening is usually acquired before writing, which requires greater cognitive and academic language. Some learners react to a new language by becoming 'silent', which can last for over a year. These learners need security and time to process the language. In the early stages listening is often in 'chunks' of language rather than in individual words.

EAL learners need planned progression for speaking and listening (EMASS 2004). The learner can try out new vocabulary and develop working knowledge of language form and structure once visual prompts and culturally familiar information are provided. Key visuals which graphically organise new knowledge give further support. Kinaesthetic activities, linked to talk, further enhance understanding. In oral learning, facial clues like intonation and gesture aid comprehension.

Many strategies which aid EAL learners help others too. Teachers need to plan for: the activation of prior knowledge; explicit modelling of talk in context; opportunities for rehearsal, repetition and clarification; thinking and reflection time to formulate speech or assimilate new language; opportunities for extended talk; linguistic prompts; and scaffolding and talk frames. Specific needs are acquisition of key language which is commonly used in speech but less in writing (like contractions, modal verbs, discourse markers and idioms and colloquialisms); for learning to be structured into manageable chunks; ideas to be expressed in more than one way; clear pronunciation; trained adults to move learners beyond the 'comfort zone'; and inclusive contexts and recognition of cultural influences.

We have to be aware that there is no 'quick fix' for the acquisition of oracy in English. It is progressive and is dependent upon the development of confidence, both in building a knowledge bank of appropriate language and in being able to use it effectively. Each learner will react differently to this challenge. By the use of careful observation and planning, all EAL learners can be supported to become secure speakers and listeners in English.

LISTENING ACTIVITIES

Activity 1: Music and thinking

Learning intention

To listen with focus and concentration, and to think of one's own ideas.

Resources

– CD player and music CD ROMs.

– Wide range of well-illustrated, colourful non-fiction books (e.g. birds, fishes, bikes, cars, machines, materials, weather, space, insects, plants, places, people . . .).

Use your favourite **instrumental** music – jazz, classical, rock. For example:

- Enya: *Amarantine*
- William Orbit: *Pieces in a Modern Style: Cavalleria Rusticana*
- Edward Elgar: *Enigma Variations*
- Respigi: *The Pines of Rome*

- Buena Vista Social Club
- Adiemus: *Songs of Sanctuary*
- Sibelius: *Lemminkainen Suite*
- Sans-Saens: *Carnival of the Animals*
- Rumillatja: *Sounds of the Andes*

Introduction

Talk to the children about *listening in class*. Tell them you know who is listening to you; ask them to say how you can tell. Ask:

- Who do *they* think is a good listener and why?
- What do they like listening to?
- What sounds don't they like?
- When is it hard to listen?
- What is the difference between hearing and listening?

Bring out the idea that we hear with our ears, but listen with our minds, and that listening helps us to think about new things we hear.

Group work

Make it clear that listening is a valuable, difficult job and that the class expects every one of the children to demonstrate their ability to listen well. Ask two children to model a talk–listen partnership; choose any topic your class is interested in, or resort to the old favourite of food: what is your favourite birthday party meal? Make it clear that during the plenary children will be asked to talk about listening.

Ask groups to choose *one* non-fiction book and within it, one picture. (You can short-cut this by providing the same picture for all groups if you prefer.) Groups now think together to write a list of six words or phrases that describe the picture.

Examples

a) picture of a red motor bike:

   describing words: red, fast, powerful, dangerous on corners, exciting, heavy

b) picture of a sparrow:

   describing words: brown, small, light, noisy, scruffy when it is wet, shy

c) picture of a stormy day:

   describing words: dark sky, thundery, strong winds, rainy, blowing trees, cold

Ask the children to *listen* to the music as it plays for about 45 seconds. When the music stops, asks groups to discuss the following:

- Do the words describe the music? Why do you think so? Can we add more words?
- If not, can we think of new words that do – perhaps opposites?

- Would the music be a good soundtrack if the picture was animated? Why/why not?

- Is there a different picture in the book that would suit the music?

- What words describe this new picture and the music?

Plenary

Ask groups to contribute their ideas about the music and its relationship to their picture.

Ask children to suggest examples of good listening, and to talk about how easy or hard it was to listen to the music, and to one another.

Ask the children for their ideas about the importance of listening, and any difficulties they experience with listening in and out of class. Help them to understand that by listening well they contribute to their own learning and, crucially, that of their classmates. Active listening means that they are helping themselves and helping each other.

Listen again to the music, this time with the ideas they have shared in mind. Use the discussion to construct a story, a picture or a poem.

Extension

Keep building up the listening time if children are responding well to this activity; listening with sustained concentration is an important skill. Children can listen for up to three minutes. They can bring in music to share. They can think creatively to link images, music and words to put together a presentation. They can reflect on and discuss music using some specific vocabulary (volume, pitch, instruments, genres of music, tone, emphasis). With no right or wrong, group interpretations depend on careful listening and shared creativity.

Activity 2: Market day

Learning intention
To listen to and follow instructions.

Resources

- **3.1 Market day** illustration (one per child).

- **Market day** picture description to read aloud.

- Coloured crayons or felt tips.

- Pencils.

3.1 Market day

Introduction

Explain that listening is very important to learning; discuss the learning intention. Tell the children that this activity will help the whole class to think about what is easy and hard about listening, and to think of some ideas to help each other listen in class.

Explain the activity:

1   To listen to the picture description, making the picture match the description.

2   To share and add own ideas to finish the picture.

Tell the children that you are going to read the description twice and that you can't stop during the reading. Check for worries about listening; is it going to be easy? Stress that there will be time for everyone to help complete the pictures after the reading is over. Importantly, explain that children are to share what they hear, that is, not 'hide' their pictures but help one another as the reading proceeds. The class can only succeed if everyone succeeds.

3.1 Market day picture description

It was market day. Right in the middle of the fruit stall was a basket with four big, juicy oranges.

Samya said, 'Two oranges please!' As she felt in her bag for her purse, she was startled by a loud cry. It was a little girl who had let go of her balloon. Up and away it went until it was only a tiny red dot in the sky.

Pavel saw the balloon too. He held on tightly to his chocolate ice cream. He loved chocolate ice cream and bought one every weekend for a treat. He went to look at the toy stall. Perhaps his sister might like a pink skipping rope?

Sitting beside the flowerbed, Herbert was feeling good. He was going to meet his friends and watch the football match.

Tom arrived at the market. He was a bit worried that it might rain. His Mum had asked him to take his baby brother out for a walk and they hadn't brought coats. He liked looking at the cloth stall. There were always rolls of coloured cloth lined up in a row. Today they all seemed to be yellow and purple.

It was very noisy at the market. A dog was barking; a plane was droning overhead; and the ice cream van was playing music. The wheels of the pushchair caught on something hard. It was a small green purse.

'Hmm!' thought Tom. 'I wonder who this belongs to!'

Group work

Read the picture description slowly and distinctly but without stopping or repeating any of it. Allow talk and comparison time. Now read the description again.

Ask the children to talk together to complete the picture, and to decide what other details they would like to add with their partner. Ask each group to make up one more 'listening sentence' that will help the class to add to the picture. Ask groups to read these out for the class to hear.

Plenary

Ask children to pass their pictures around; or ask children to move around the room looking at one another's work; provide post-it notes for children to leave a positive comment on the work of their classmates.

Ask one group to describe problems with listening. Ask this group to select other children to contribute. Bring out the children's concerns about listening in class, in the hall, in school generally. Ask for suggestions on how to deal with these problems.

Extension

Display the pictures. Ask each group to write a short story about their picture, or to act out a scene starting with the picture.

Create a 'listening' display: animals with big ears: children listening: speech bubbles with 'listening and hearing' vocabulary; have a corner with things to listen to – audio books, toys which generate sound; make links between listening, thinking and speaking: link to Science 4 topic of sound; link to work in music.

Organise good listening awards or star charts.

Keep *listening* on the class agenda as a talking point for other lessons. Create other pictures and read out related information to support curriculum work.

Use plenary sessions to help children reflect on the mechanics of, and the importance of, listening. Who is a good listener? Who is improving? Who finds it difficult, and how can we help? Why do we need to listen? What's the difference between listening and active listening?

Activity 3: Internet shopping on Mars

Learning intention
To listen and remember; sharing memories with others.

Resources
- **Internet shopping on Mars** story.
- **3.2 Internet shopping list**.

Introduction
Tell the children that they are going to use their memories, and check that everyone knows what that means. Do the children know how important memory is, and do they consider themselves to have good memories? Ask how we put things in our memories; bring out the idea that we can hear and remember. Stress the importance of listening.

Explain the idea that *the class has a memory*; that by listening and thinking together, the class can recall and describe events and activities – and learning – which any one individual may not be able to recall in such detail alone. Think of an example. What did your class do in a particularly memorable session the previous week, month or term? By reflecting and sharing ideas aloud, and listening to one another, children can recall incidents and what they learned in surprising detail. Children benefit from raised awareness of this whole-class ability – the recall of common knowledge. It explains why and how we teach in whole-class settings; why every class member is important, and how knowledge and understanding are generated and consolidated over the school year (Edwards and Mercer 1987).

The class are going to hear a story and remember some details. **Internet shopping on Mars** provides rhythmic and alphabetical clues to aid memory. You can use any suitable story, later asking children to recall names, events and what characters did and said and looked like.

Group work

Read the story once. Allow talk time, asking children to recall and share what they heard; provide **3.2 Internet shopping list**; then read the story again.

Ask groups to talk together to fill in the shopping list sheet with pictures of the things that the Martians wanted and complete the word list of items for each character.

Plenary

Ask the class to share their versions of the story. Build up a joint version before reading the 'official' version again. Which items were easy to recall; which were more difficult? Can children suggest a classmate who seemed to remember detail well?

Ask children to think about how we use memory to help us learn. Bring out the idea that the class has a joint memory of shared events, activities and instructions, and that if we all share what we remember, we will all do better in class. Give a further example – ask children to recall a detail from a lesson in the previous week. Ask the children to think about how different it would be if everything in class was a competition; and assure them that it isn't.

Extension

Ask children to write their own alphabetical shopping list. Choose one of these lists to repeat this lesson.

Check if the class can remember shopping items the next day or the following week.

Play the game **'I went on holiday and . . .'**. Children sit in a circle. First child says, I went on holiday and I took *swimming goggles* – i.e. one item. Next child says, I went on holiday and we took swimming goggles and a camera. Next child says, I went on holiday and we took swimming goggles and a camera and some chocolate buttons – and so on.

3.2 Internet shopping on Mars story

Quixa and Zoozo, who lived on Mars, were playing Earth Invaders on their computer. 'Let's have a look on the Internet,' said Zoozo. 'Check out all the strange things you can have on Earth.'

'I want to travel, and I want something nice to eat, and some toys, and something to wear,' said Quixa.

'Well, we can write a shopping list for when we win the Interplanetary Lottery,' said Zoozo.

They looked around the Internet shopping pages on their screens.

'Ok!' said Quixa. 'This is my list.'

– air tickets	– X Box	– stripy cat
– biscuits	– yoyo	– woolly hat

Quixa had just found a woolly hat with special holes for antennae when their Mum appeared. 'I want some things from the Internet too,' she said. 'Can you really get anything you want?'

'Yup!' said Zoozo. 'What sort of things do you mean?'

This was Mum's Internet shopping list.

– DVD	– envelopes	– free range eggs
– violin	– umbrella	– tent pegs

'Right you are,' said Zoozo. 'There's some stuff I'd like to look at too. I want a pet, and some sweets. Look, this is my list –.'

– ginger beer	– hamster	– ice-cream
– Smarties	– roller blades	– plasticene

News of the Internet shopping list had got around, and Granny appeared. 'What about me?' she said. 'I'd look myself, but I just spilt a cup of green tea on my laptop and it won't work!'

'Ok . . .' said Quixa, keying in the strange things on Granny's list.

– jam	– kite	– lava light
– orange juice	– newspaper	– marmite

Dad appeared. 'Are we shopping or wishing?' he said. 'Anyway, I only want two things – a quad bike and a zodiac map.'

'Ok, then, that's the lot,' said Quixa, typing rapidly. 'One for every letter of the alphabet. My cat's going to be called Tabs. What will you call your hamster?'

Zoozo had obviously thought about this already. 'Google,' he said.

3.2 Internet shopping on Mars story

a	b	c	d
e	f	g	h
i	j	k	l
m	n	o	p
q	r	s	t
u	v	w	x
y	z		

The aliens' lists:

Quixa _____

Zozoo _____

Dad _____

Mum _____

Granny _____

What our group would like to buy from Mars:

_____

_____

_____

_____

If needed, the children can have 'thinking time' first to decide on their item; or can be given a card with an item on; or can be given a letter of the alphabet that their item must start with; or can work in pairs to support one another.

Activity 4: Making a working leaf

Learning intention
To listen to others in class; sharing understanding

Resources
Use **3.3 Making a working leaf**.

–   Six different kinds of leaves from trees or shrubs (for a class of 30, grouped in 6 groups of 5, you will need at least 10 of each sort of leaf).

–   Centimetre squared paper.

–   Small amount of brown or white sugar.

–   Straws.

–   Gold or yellow paper.

–   Green highlighters.

–   Blue, black and red crayons.

–   Pencils.

–   Glue.

–   Scissors.

–   Calculators.

–   Name lists (put children in groups of five or six; each child needs a list of names of the others in their group).

Introduction
Explain that listening to one another is really important if everyone is to do well. At the end of the lesson you will be asking for examples of good listening.

3.3 Making a working leaf

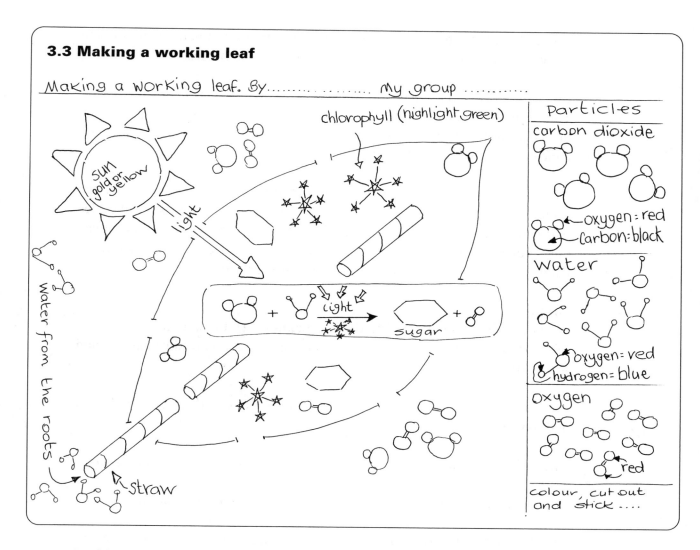

Making a working leaf. By................ .... my group ....

In this activity, everyone will make a model of a working leaf, and gain an understanding of how leaves work. Explain this, then ask everyone to think hard and see if they can tell their talk partner, what is the job of a leaf? That is, what do leaves do, or why do plants have leaves?

After time to talk and listen, choose a starter child to share ideas with the class. Ask this child to choose another and so on, until the class builds up a range of ideas of what a leaf is and does. At this stage, there is no need to comment on the ideas or do anything but encourage their expression, and ensure that all are listening.

Group work 1

Divide the class into six groups of five. Tell the children that they are going to find out how big a leaf is – that is, how much it spreads out, or what its surface area is. Provide each child in a group with two leaves, centimetre squared paper, pencils and scissors. A group should all have the same kind of leaves. Each child should draw round their leaves, cut out the shape, and then count the squares; add together halves and quarters to make whole boxes.

Colour boxes if it helps accuracy. Early finishers should help others in their group. Record the areas of the leaves in a list next to names.

Using the calculators, add up the numbers. Now divide by the number of leaves. This gives an average leaf area in square centimetres. Ask the groups to stick their cut-out leaves on coloured paper and record the average leaf area, with their names, and if possible the name of the sort of leaf.

Now ask the class to listen again. Ask a member of each group to give the average leaf area of their type of leaf. Ask the children to consider the idea that leaves have a large surface area for their size; that they are very spread out. They are this shape for a reason; their job is to catch sunlight. Hold out hands to show how spreading out can increase surface area.

Group work 2

Provide each child with **3.3 Making a working leaf**. Look at the illustrations of carbon dioxide and oxygen, and explain that these are invisible gases found in the air.

Make sure everyone knows which colours to use to colour carbon, hydrogen and oxygen.

Check for understanding of these words: *dissolve; chemical; invisible; energy*.

Choose *ten* children to read out the following items of information.

Ask the class to *listen carefully*, finding the things mentioned on their picture:

Description of what a leaf does

1 Carbon dioxide and oxygen are invisible gases, found in the air all around the leaf.

2 The leaf lets air inside itself through small holes on the underside.

3 The leaf gets water from the plant's roots through long tubes.

4 Leaves contain a green-coloured chemical called chlorophyll.

5 The green colour soaks up light energy from the sun, and the job of the leaf is to store this trapped energy in a high-energy chemical, called sugar.

6 To make sugar, the leaf mixes carbon dioxide and water together, and adds in energy from the sunlight.

7 As well as sugar, the leaf makes oxygen, which escapes from the leaf into the air.

8 The sugar that the leaf makes is food for the whole plant to grow and live.

9 Sugar dissolves easily. The plant changes sugar into starch, because otherwise rain would wash its sugar away.

10 Animals eat plants because they need sugar to live, and they can't make their own like plants can.

Ask children to say what they heard. Encourage children to express ideas in their own words without spending too long on this or insisting on absolute accuracy. Now explain that the groups are going to help each other finish the picture. Ask the children to *listen* to the instructions.

Instructions for using 3.3 Making a working leaf

1 Colour and stick on the carbon dioxide, water and oxygen.

2 Stick on the straw for water.

3 Use shiny or yellow paper to make the sun, and the light arrow.

4 Highlight the chlorophyll green.

5 Stick sugar in the hexagon (**CARE!** Remind children that kitchen chemicals in classrooms are not to be eaten because they may be poisonous and cause tummy upsets!).

6 If finished early, help others; colour the leaf pale green; draw animals (e.g. caterpillars) eating the leaf.

Some children may like to know that this process is *photosynthesis* ('light used for making').

During group work provide both the Instructions and Description list above on the IWB, a poster or an A4 sheet so that children have access to the written words as well as being able to discuss what they are doing.

Plenary

Ask groups to talk together to decide how a leaf works – what it does and why.

> A leaf traps light energy using chlorophyll. It uses this energy, carbon dioxide and water to make sugar. Sunlight energy is stored in sugar and starch. Leaves also make oxygen as a waste product, which it lets out into the air. Plants have energy to grow because they make their own food like this. Animals cannot make sugar. Plants support animal life.

Choose a child to start telling the class their ideas. Reinforce accurate ideas. Ask for contributions or corrections. Ask for children to choose the next contributor to build up a clear idea of the job of a leaf. Finally, ask the groups to decide why their leaves are so big and flat. Ask for class contributions to support the idea of a large surface area to 'catch' sunlight and allow carbon dioxide in and oxygen out.

Tell the children to make sure they ask their parents the starter question when they go home; do you know why trees have leaves? This might give the child another chance to articulate their understanding.

Remind the children of the learning intention, and how important listening was in this lesson. Ask them for examples of good listening. Also ask children to decide who was helpful in the groups. This lesson can demonstrate that good listening and collaboration means that everyone learns well. Ask the children to reflect on their learning. What have they learned by listening?

Extension

Provide photocopies of the ten statements, cut up and mixed up. Ask groups to sequence these correctly, to illustrate and stick in their books, or make a poster, adding their **Working leaf** pictures.

Listening ideas

Use learning intentions for active listening for the whole class, or target specific individual needs. Use in conjunction with curriculum learning intentions. Review progress in your plenary session, asking children to provide examples of effective listening and learning.

Play a traffic lights game during P.E. and transfer this into the classroom:

- Using coloured cards: red = stop, orange = listen, green = go.

- Using sound: one whistle = stop, clap hands = listen, double whistle = go.

Mobile conversation: ask children to take on characters from a current story book and make up a mobile phone conversation to share with the class.

Dictation: if used with a 'listening' learning intention, a paragraph containing class spellings, science vocabulary, new or interesting words, can be read out for children to either write down or check off on a list.

Children can make a sound tape at home, to share with the class, recording a variety of sounds. Children working in groups listen, share ideas and identify what they hear.

Create a display of sound words, for example:

- **Volume**: noisy, loud, quiet.

- **Pitch**: high, low.

- **Rhythm**: regular, irregular.

- **Instruments**: percussion, stringed, wind.

- **Music**: tune, rhythm, beat, tempo, waltz, march.

- **Noisy machines**: car, lorry, tractor, motorbike, lawnmower, television.

- **Pleasant sounds**: bird song, singing, laughter, kettle boiling.

Ask children to collect pictures of sound sources (trumpet, piano, people talking, machines) to add to the display. Add describing words for each sound, or onomatopoeia words (*Crash! Squelch! Scrunch!*) using comics as a source.

Display pictures of animal ears with emphasis on the difference between hearing (passive) and listening (active). Consider why hearing is a vital sense for animals and humans.

Use the British Library Sound Archives comprehensive collection of animal sounds, rainstorms, Victorian street – everything – to enrich presentations and for 'listening' quizzes.

Look at hearing impairment and the ways people have found to get round problems over the ages. Make the most of the link with science work on sound.

Ensure that your voice is not over-used. Use recordings of stories and sounds instead of reading yourself. Use sound signals to indicate when the class should stop or pack up. Save your energy and the impact your voice has for learning conversations and for more personal talk with individuals in your class.

Research and discuss the impact of body language with the class. How accurately can we convey meaning without words?

Summary

Children listen in class if they are interested, if they understand what is happening, and if they know how and why to listen. We can generate activities focused on listening in order to provide children with chances to discuss and come to recognise the importance of listening in classrooms. Children who have had such opportunities are likely to see the force of requests for them to listen; if they know that by doing so, they will learn more themselves and help others to learn, they may be motivated to try. Interestingly, listening carefully can help children to become *more* motivated, by being drawn in to thinking and engaging with classroom activities. Closing plenary sessions offer invaluable opportunities to discuss what difference active listening can make to understanding; what problems people have with listening, particularly in a large group; how to help others listen; and so on. Active listening is a life skill and all children benefit from an awareness of their own capacity to use it.

Further reading

EMASS (2004) *Supporting Pupils with English as an Additional Language*. EMASS: Milton Keynes.

Hadfield, J. and Hadfield, C. (2006) *Simple Listening Activities*. Oxford: Oxford University Press.

CHAPTER 4

Dialogic teaching

Orchestrating effective dialogue in whole-class sessions

> Dialogic teaching harnesses the power of talk to engage children, stimulate and extend their thinking, and advance learning and understanding.
>
> (Alexander 2006: 37)

> The emphasis upon language for performance rather than for exploration is, of course, communicated by many teachers when they treat classroom discussion as an opportunity for cross questioning.
>
> (Barnes 1992: 61)

Children's questions, their tentative thoughts and hypothetical ideas, supply the energy for their learning. How can we ensure that children are prepared to express uncertainty, offer newly formed and uncertain ideas, and consider the ideas of others as things to be challenged and tested out loud? Our talk with children – the way we teach – is the most important tool we have available for teaching and learning. Whether or not children think and learn through talk in your classroom depends on your awareness of how you use language to interact. This brings us to the concept of *dialogic teaching*. Teachers and children, through dialogue, can work towards understanding, using and learning valuable strategies for thinking.

Dialogic teaching can be thought of as a 'syndrome' – a combination of various conditions that build up into a recognisable teaching approach. Dialogic teaching was identified and described by eminent educational researcher Robin Alexander, based on analysis of his detailed observations of classroom life:

> Dialogic teaching deals not just with what is to be learned, but how. It explores the learner's thought processes.
>
> (Alexander 2006: 35)

Alexander describes *teaching* that leads to dialogue in classroom discussions, and ultimately to deeper learning. Can we analyse our own teaching and discern patterns that Alexander identifies in others? Can we see the benefits of dialogue and ensure that these benefits are achieved in our own classroom on an everyday basis?

What is dialogic teaching?

Dialogic teaching means finding out what children think, engaging with their developing ideas and helping them to talk through misunderstandings.

When children are given opportunities to contribute to extended classroom dialogue they can explore the limits of their own understanding. At the same time they can practise new ways of using language as a tool for constructing knowledge.

By engaging children in dialogue, teachers can:

- elicit children's ideas;
- explain ideas;
- clarify the point and purpose of what the children will do in class;
- model or demonstrate useful ways of using language;
- help children grasp new concepts and new ways to describe their thoughts.

The teacher's role in encouraging listening, speaking and thinking is crucial. The teacher provides stimulus by asking genuine questions and encouraging children to do the same. There is a linked flow of talk with ideas building on one another to create a bigger, deeper or more detailed picture than any one child will have thought of alone. Points are taken up, examined and challenged. Ideas can be tentative and hypothetical, or in need of some modification.

During dialogic teaching children offer longer contributions, with everyone actively listening and responding. The class, as an audience, is open, attentive and challenging without being threatening. A feature of dialogic teaching is that children are given time to think. Time to think can seem like empty space; silence for as little as ten seconds can seem interminable in a classroom. Children can be directly taught what to do with their minds in this time.

Dialogic teaching allows teachers to have access to children's ideas. These may be deeply held or transient; either way, dialogue enables teachers to move on children's thinking. During dialogue, children have an unusual opportunity to hear and consider new information, opinions and questions. They literally have the chance to 'change their minds' by matching their thinking against that of others. Subject learning is developed as new ideas are put forward, challenged and generally mulled over. It is an opportunity to develop curiosity about the thoughts of others and the capacity to reflect.

Children also learn that this sort of talk with other people can help them to both understand and question things. With their classmates, as they practise dialogue, children can see how ideas can be generated and questioned in order to test and make sense of them. They can then think this way when working alone through a problem or new set of ideas. They can learn to see that there are reasons why people think differently. This is a step on the way to tolerance, understanding and negotiating compromise.

Indicators of dialogic teaching

Towards Dialogic Teaching (Alexander 2006) sets out to establish a description of what dialogic teaching can be like in practice, with the intention of provoking and informing a debate about what constitutes effective teaching. As teachers, we can join in this debate to offer informed comment on key issues such as the role of the teacher, the fundamental nature of classroom talk in children's learning and the impact that dialogic teaching might be expected to have.

Among the most significant indicators of dialogic teaching are:

- Questions are structured so as to encourage thoughtful answers.

- Answers stimulate further questions and are seen as the building blocks of a longer dialogue, rather than end points.

- The teacher chains contributions into a coherent whole, helping children to discern meaning and think of new questions.

Indicators in teacher talk

Dialogic teaching involves talk in which:

- questions are structured to provoke thoughtful answers;

- answers provoke further questions;

- exchanges are chained into coherent lines of enquiry;

- there is a balance between encouraging participation and extending understanding;

- pupils ask questions and provide explanations;

- turns are managed by shared routines rather than 'bidding';

- those who are not speaking are actively participating;

- the classroom is organised to encourage listening, looking, reflecting and evaluating;

- everyone speaks clearly, audibly and expressively;

- children understand the importance of the discussion;

- children have the confidence to make mistakes.

Indicators in children's talk

Every child attends, and children:

- narrate;

- explain;

- instruct;

- ask different kinds of questions;

- receive, act and build upon answers;

- analyse and solve problems;

- speculate and imagine;

- explore and evaluate ideas;

- discuss;

- argue, reason and justify;

- negotiate.

In summary, dialogic teaching is:

- *Collective:* teachers and children address learning tasks together.

- *Reciprocal*: teachers and children listen to each other, share ideas and consider alternative viewpoints.

- *Supportive:* children articulate their ideas freely and help one another to reach common understandings.

- *Cumulative:* ideas are chained into coherent lines of enquiry.

- *Purposeful:* teachers plan dialogic teaching with particular educational goals in view.

(Adapted from Alexander 2006: pp. 28, 37–43)

Guest Speaker: Harry Daniels, Professor of Education, Centre for Sociocultural and Activity Theory Research, University of Bath

Language as a pedagogic tool

People speak in ways that are specific to the context in which they are speaking. For example, mothers speak in particular ways to their babies; pupils and teachers speak to each other in ways that reflect the nature of the curriculum context. Speakers are not simply constrained and determined by the context in which they are speaking, they also shape and transform that context and the ways in which practices of communication are enacted. From this point of view, speech may be seen as a construction, a device or artefact that mediates, or goes between people and the places in which they speak.

Speech and forms of speaking are social creations that carry the histories of their use and are tools for the creation of new meanings. When contexts change or are changed, new forms of speech arise. This happens as children learn and develop, as well as when historical, social change takes place.

Speaking always involves the negotiation of meaning. However much politicians and the popular press would like us to believe that simply structuring and sequencing instruction guarantee learning, social and cultural psychologists have shown how every response to teaching is best thought of as a creative response. The very act of negotiation of meaning and dialogue that underpins modern understandings of communication, including pedagogic communication, denies the 'magic bullet' or direct, unmediated notion of instruction.

Communication with signs, perhaps especially speech, becomes the central concern for teachers as they seek to help children acquire and develop new understandings. Ways of talking, thinking and making meaning are intertwined. Teaching involves helping others to get involved with new ways of thinking. Learners need the tools that are required to do this new form of 'work'. When seen as a pedagogic tool, language is perhaps the most important focus of the practice of teaching. It is both the object on which teaching should focus – we should work on helping learners to participate in new ways of talking – and also the tool with which learners work on their own thinking and the thinking of others.

STRATEGIES FOR DIALOGIC TEACHING

1 Eliciting ideas in lesson introductions and conclusions

1a Introduction recap

Context: whole-class introduction during an ongoing topic. Provide key vocabulary. Ask groups to talk together to summarise previous lessons or recall what they experienced. Each group is then asked for a sentence saying what they have learned or understood; the teacher invites one group to contribute, moving round the groups until all feel that the summary of previous work is complete. During this summary, the child who is speaking may ask others in the room to contribute or comment.

1b Lesson conclusion – reflection

Context: whole-class closing plenary. Ask groups to talk together to agree on:

- a sentence about something they learned and how they learned it;

- a question about some aspect of the work;

- something they did not understand or would like to learn more about;

- a suggestion for what they may need to revise;

- a suggestion for what they think would be useful or interesting to do next.

Invite groups to offer their ideas. Questions can be answered by other groups or individuals, and similar or contrasting viewpoints noted.

1c Nomination

Context: whole-class dialogue session. A child who has just contributed to the whole-class discussion is asked to *nominate* the next child to speak. They may also think up a question for the person they have nominated. You may need to rephrase some responses to help things along, or chain ideas so that they link up. While children are learning how and why the turn-taking of nomination works, it may also be necessary to ask children to make their choice from another group or boy/girl to ensure that everyone has the chance to speak. Nomination is a very good strategy for getting away from the constraints of teacher questions and brief answers, with children bidding for turns with hands up.

2 Planning talk-based activities – 'Now let's talk about it . . .'

Context: group work. Children can talk and think together, aware that they will be asked to explain and give reasons for their jointly agreed ideas.

Activities that stimulate productive talk

Concept maps. A concept map is a graphic representation of how an individual or group understands or thinks. Concept maps can be used to examine thinking about a topic or for a story the class is reading. The ability to construct and use concept maps can be built up in stages:

1 Provide pairs or groups with key words arranged so that the links between them become apparent. Ask groups to discuss how the key words are linked – that is, to explain their conception relationships between ideas. Draw lines to show links.

2 Children discuss which word, phrase or sentence can be written along linking lines to describe the relationship.

3 Provide up to twelve key words on cards and ask groups to discuss how to arrange them so that linked concepts are physically near to one another before linking lines and relationship words are added.

4 Children discuss and choose their own key words and create mind maps.

Concept maps can help children to share their ideas, so that their reasoning is apparent. Gaps or errors in understanding become evident through differences of opinion. Areas of uncertainty can be highlighted, discussed with the whole class, and form the basis of subsequent teaching.

Collecting information. Each group is given a relevant item of information, picture or object to talk and think about. One child leaves their group, visits another group, talks with them about their information (etc.), then returns to their own group and recounts or explains what they have been told or shown. The children discuss this input before a different child visits another group.

Whole-class work sharing. During group activity, ask one person at a time to leave their group and take a minute or two to visit others around the room, looking at their work, offering positive comments and sharing ideas about it. During the plenary, invite children to give examples of effective work of others, or say how this helped their own work.

Group mix. Give each group a number. Provide each child in a group with a different coloured sticker. Once group work is under way, ask (for example) all 'orange' children to move to the group with the *next* number. Ensure that they are welcomed and that the group's work so far is explained. Once groups are established and working again, if time, ask (for example) 'green' children to move to the group with the *previous* number. Again, the group explains and describes its work before continuing. Finally, all children return to their original group. As well as asking children to show what they have learned, ask for comments on the experience of re-grouping – advantages, surprises, problems. There may be particular value in asking those who did not move to describe the effect of changes on learning and their impression of being the 'anchor' for the group.

Group consequences. These are effective when drafting text, problem solving or planning an enquiry. Provide an activity in which children discuss their ideas with their group and then work individually on separate paper/books/computer pages. Once work is underway, ask children to swap papers/computers etc., look at what is there, discuss and continue. Once enough time has elapsed, exchange again with a different member of the group to make sure that everyone has contributed to each other's work. If possible, you can also ask children to choose another person in the class they would like to exchange with. Finally, return the work to its original 'owner' to look at and complete. Ask groups to think together to evaluate the shared work and decide how contributions helped. It may be that some contributions were not wanted, allowing the child or group to clarify what they did want.

Talking Points (see Chapter 2)
Talking Points help children to prepare for whole-class dicussion. Examples of Talking Points are **4.1 Magnetism** and **4.2 The Deserted House**.

4.1 Talking Points: Magnetism

Talk with your group to find out what everyone thinks, and agree on your ideas. Are these points true, false, or are you unsure? Please give REASONS for your ideas.

1 Magnets have poles. The north pole of a magnet points north.

2 The earth is a magnet because it is made of metal inside.

3 Magnets pull metal things but not all metals are magnetic.

4 Magnetism is a force.

5 Magnetism is strongest near the ends of magnets.

7 Magnets always point in the same direction if free to move.

8 Steel can act as a barrier to a magnetic field.

9 You can make magnetism from electricity.

10 Magnets don't work under water.

11 Magnets attract each other and repel each other.

12 We get the word magnet from the metal magnesium.

13 A compass needle is a magnet that turns as the earth turns.

14 If you cut a magnet in half, you get two magnets.

15 Magnets can be any shape at all.

16 Magnets are just toys.

17 Round magnets do not have poles.

18 Magnets don't work through paper.

19 Magnetic force is all round a magnet, not just at the poles.

20 The earth's north magnetic pole is at the actual North Pole in the Arctic.

Now draw a cartoon to show how magnets work. What would a magnetic character look like?

4.2 Talking Points: 'The Deserted House'

Read the poem. Discuss the talking points. Ask everyone for their ideas and reasons, before deciding what your group agrees.

The Deserted House
Mary Coleridge

There's no smoke in the chimney,
And the rain beats on the floor;
There's no glass in the window,
There's no wood in the door;
The heather grows behind the house,
And the sand lies before.

No hand has trained the ivy,
The walls are grey and bare;
The boats upon the sea sail by,
Nor ever tarry here.
No beast of the field comes nigh,
Nor any bird of the air.

Word meanings: **tarry**: stay a while; **comes nigh**: comes near

Talking Points

1   This poem was written a long time ago.

2   It's a big house in the north of England.

3   The house is in a field near a town.

4   The house burnt down.

5   The poem is about a painting of a house.

6   'Beasts of the field' means sheep.

7   Something in the house is keeping the birds away.

8   The house has only recently been deserted.

9   It is a haunted house on an island.

10   Its owners won the lottery and moved to a bigger house.

11   The people left because . . .

12   What will happen next is . . .

Draw a picture of the house. Use the words of the poem and your own words to label your picture.

3 Assessing children's understanding through speaking and listening

Discussion can aid assessment by bringing out misconceptions or areas of uncertainty. Everything a child says is an opportunity to assess their thinking and learning.

3a Talk about examination questions

Formal assessment is full of pitfalls for children. Their understanding – or otherwise – of what the question is actually asking them can affect the clarity and accuracy of their response. Through discussion, we can help children to understand what is really wanted. This is not 'teaching to the tests' which means selectively teaching children specific factual knowledge. Encouraging children to reflect on, discuss and evaluate questions and articulate a range of ideas about possible answers calls into play higher order thinking skills. Children need to know how to answer paper-based questions.

- Provide each child with a paper-based question to complete alone; collect in and mark.

- Using the same question, ask children to talk through their ideas with you or a teaching assistant. Ask them to explain the thinking behind their answers. Would your understanding of their thinking affect their mark?

- Ask groups to look at the question and share their ideas about what it is asking without writing anything down.

- Ask children to contribute to a whole-class discussion of a question, ensuring that uncertainties are aired and those who initially answered the question inaccurately have the chance to say what they think and respond to the different ideas of others.

3b Evaluating the work of others

Provide groups of children with examples of class work, preferably anonymous work from another class. Help them to understand marking criteria by asking groups to decide what is 'good' work; list the things that make the work good. Discuss the need to focus on specific aspects of the work. For example, will spelling and handwriting matter?

4.3 My choice plan

My name is _____

I want to work with _____

I am not going to work with _____

My plan

I am going to _____

Because _____

_____

_____

Time I am going to take _____

What else I might need to make my work good _____

_____

_____

What I already know about this _____

Some questions I want to answer _____

My review

What I did _____

What I found out _____

These are the answers to the questions _____

What I would like to do next _____

What I will need to help me _____

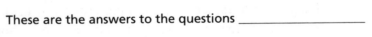

Dialogic teaching

- In discussion with a partner, mark the work provided using agreed criteria.

- Decide what help the person needs if they are to improve.

- Mark a different sample of work. Check if the mark matches that of the original markers. Discuss any discrepancies.

- Repeat the process using samples of their own work.

3c Assessing motivation

Learning is intricately bound up with motivation; how interesting is the topic to the child? Set out resources for three or more activities related to your on-going topics. Ask children to choose which to use. Start by recording briefly what they want to do or find out; that is, make a plan using **4.3 My choice plan**.

Provide time to use the resources. Afterwards, ask children to talk with you or to one another to evaluate their current thinking; how does this match with their plan?

Ask them to think and record their plan for what to do next.

4 Giving children time to think

Context: whole-class discussion.

Ask children not to raise their hands. Talk to them to set out the problem, ideas or questions for discussion. Ask the children to think alone for a minute or so, then share ideas with those nearby. Remind everyone that the class learning depends on active listening. Now ask a child by name to contribute. Build thinking time into the ensuing discussion by asking children not to put up their hands; then wait a few moments after they have spoken before asking another child to speak.

Context: at the computer.

Use an on-screen timer or conventional sand timer. Ask each group to ensure that they think about the problem, their writing and so on, for a set length of time before moving on.

Dialogic teaching in practice

Encouraging classroom talk can cause problems. Children may not listen to one another; some children may never contribute; others may be overly aggressive when challenging or challenged. Some barriers can be overcome by planning, for example:

- Make explicit the ground rules that govern talk in the classroom by teaching children about the purpose of their talk with you and their classmates.

- Analyse the talk that has gone on, asking children to evaluate its quality and impact.

- Establish a talk focus and a 'thinking' atmosphere, valuing contributions, and asking questions to which you really do not know the answer.

- Discuss with children their role as listeners. Not all voices can be heard because there is not enough time. You can find out what the children think about this, and ask for their suggestions for 'fairer' turn-taking. Find out who they like to listen to.

- Ask confident children to talk about their perceptions of class talk. Compare with the views of quieter children.

- Have a 'dialogue star'. Choose a child who is expected to make the initial contribution and change every week so each child in class eventually takes this role.

- Use talk partners and groups so that questions and ideas can be shared with someone, if not with everyone.

Dialogue has the potential to wander off into uncharted territory. Decide in advance how much freedom is useful, interesting or helpful. Sometimes the answer is none, and it is fine to keep the learning intention clearly in focus. Sometimes there is chance to explore. Help the children to recognise what sort of discussion you expect, and teach them how to elaborate on their ideas and those of others.

Time your discussions carefully – stop while you are winning. Some children may want to continue to talk about the topic with you later; some may take their thoughts away for reflection or discussion at home. Teach the children that conclusions cannot always be reached.

Distractions are a universal classroom worry and individual behaviour problems another, because of their impacts on learning. The dialogic classroom offers the child the security of knowing that their ideas are important and that their voice will be heard. In addition, class ground rules for talk mean that the whole process makes more sense. Talk which has a real point can be more interesting than the everyday distractions children devise for one another.

Reviewing your work space and teaching strategies to encourage dialogue

Classroom organisation

- Where can the children sit so that they can see one another as well as possible?

- Where can you stand or sit to be visible and to orchestrate the talk?

- Will moving tables and chairs create an atmosphere more suitable for talk?

Learning intentions

- Are the children aware of the learning intentions for the topic and for their talk?

- Is it really necessary to write out the learning intentions?

- Do children know how dialogue can help achieve learning intentions?

Your talk with the children

- Does your planning include time for you to involve children in a dialogue with you and each other?

- Have you planned 'why', 'how' or 'what do you think' questions to help initiate dialogue?

- Are you and the class prepared to continue a line of thinking with an individual child?

- Does your class understand the importance of extended responses?

- Are children willing to share tentative thoughts with you and one another, admitting errors and asking questions?

- Can members of your class talk to one another, examining ideas and following a line of reasoning, with you in support?

- Do all children in your class have the confidence, ability and motivation to speak and listen during whole-class discussions?

- Do you use what happens during the lesson to think of some plenary questions that will help children to think aloud, building on one another's responses?

Children's awareness of talk for learning

- Are the ground rules that help to generate and sustain whole-class dialogue transparent to the children, commonly talked about and open to review?

- Can the children evaluate the effectiveness of their group and whole-class talk? Do they have the understanding and vocabulary to do so, and do they know how important this is?

- Do the children understand that learning is a whole-class enterprise and that if one person is uncertain, the whole class cannot succeed unless they help?

A learning dialogue

Teachers have a wide range of techniques – for example, they explain, question, describe and instruct – depending on what they are trying to achieve. Teaching episodes taken out of context may not allow us to understand what is happening in a classroom, but we can each consider and evaluate our own teaching style, aiming to achieve a range of talk-focused strategies and an overall balance in which dialogic teaching episodes are thoughtfully and frequent used.

The following exchange, *Degrees Celsius*, occurred in a Year 6 classroom. The class were using thermometers to measure warm water cooling and temperature change when crushed ice was mixed with salt. Their comments revealed gaps in factual knowledge; many did not know key temperatures on the Celsius scale. The teacher provided pictures of a thermometer and asked children to mark: *zero degrees* – water freezes; *100 degrees* – water boils; *20 degrees* – room temperature. The whole class then shared their ideas.

Degrees Celsius

Teacher	What do you think is your body temperature?
Karen	37 degrees.
Teacher	37 degrees Celsius, right.
Suri	So you are a lot warmer than room temperature.
Ben	Warmer? No, but . . . can't be right otherwise we would be cooling down all the time.
Teacher	You're right, yes we are. That's why we wear clothes, to keep us warm.
Ben	No, um, things end up the same temperature, like, the water is [*referring to the water cooling from sixty to twenty degrees*].
Teacher	Room temperature is twenty degrees-ish, we are about thirty-seven, like Karen said, unless you are a lizard.

Ben	No . . . where does that heat come from?
Teacher	Well, there are lots, there are reactions going on in your cells, all the time, that give out heat. You are a source of heat. Your food, you use food as fuel and you burn it up to move and breathe and – make heat.
Ben	Ah.

Comment. Ben, surprised by the difference between room and body temperature, had the confidence to challenge information offered by the teacher. To do so – three times – with reasons, is commendable and indicates that there is trust between teacher and class. The dialogue that Ben initiated contributed to the learning of his classmates.

Summary

Too often educational change is externally imposed and it's the thankless task of the teacher to try to make 'innovation' work in practice. However, change towards dialogic teaching can be a personal goal. The benefits for children as individuals, for the class as a unit, for everyone's learning and for our own job satisfaction are evident. Listening to children, discussing their ideas in ways that help them make meaning together, and showing them how best to use their minds and their spoken language, are all reasons why we enlist as teachers in the first place. Dialogic teaching, as its name says quite clearly, is the responsibility of the teacher. Its outcomes for teachers include finding out what children really think and being able to teach them what they need to know, honestly and clearly. Its outcomes for children are a deeper engagement with learning, and a better understanding of how and why they should talk with everyone in their class.

They should also have time to think. Isn't this what we want in our classrooms?

Further reading

Alexander, R. J. (2006) *Towards Dialogic Teaching: Rethinking Classroom Talk.* York: Dialogos. (First edition 2004.)

Mercer, N. (1995) *The Guided Construction of Knowledge.* Clevedon: Multilingual Matters.

Mercer, N. and Littleton, K. (2007) *Dialogue and the Development of Children's Thinking.* London: Routledge.

Group work

Ensuring that all children collaborate in educationally effective group work

> If it can be shown that groups can *learn* to elaborate, this
> would be an important educational finding.
>
> (Barnes 1992: 66)

Speaking and listening in groups

We can teach children how and why they can have a good discussion; every
one of them can learn to contribute, reason, elaborate and generally think aloud
with others. Collaborative working is not created by seating arrangements,
but by teaching children why and how they should talk to one another during
class activities. It's easy for them to wander off task when they are talking
during group work. It is crucial to give children the understanding and skills
they need to defer social talk *without creating conflict*. They must know how
to agree and how to disagree by showing that it is the idea or opinion they
wish to challenge, not the speaker. This is essential learning.

This chapter suggests activities for the direct teaching of talk based on the
'Thinking Together' approach. Thinking Together has been shown to raise
achievement in curriculum areas such as literacy, numeracy, science and
citizenship where discussion takes place (Mercer, Wegerif & Dawes 1999).

Teaching Thinking Together

To take part in group discussion, children need to:

a) understand the link between speaking, listening and learning;

b) have created and agreed whole-class ground rules for exploratory talk;

c) know some speaking and listening strategies for discussion.

Guest Speaker: Neil Mercer, Professor of Education, University of Cambridge

The importance of teaching speaking and listening

Two or more people working together can achieve more than the sum of their individual contributions. Language is designed for doing something much more interesting than transmitting information accurately from one person to another: it enables individual minds to be combined in a collective, communicative intelligence, so that people can make better sense of the world and devise practical ways of dealing with it. Language enables people jointly to create new ideas and reflect on them. With language, we can not only 'interact', we can 'interthink'. Helping children to understand why people succeed or fail in using talk for thinking together should be an important function of classroom education.

Teachers can agree on what constitutes good group work and effective speaking and listening, but it seems that such discussion is rare in classrooms. Recordings capture talk in which children don't listen to each other, in which one person dominates the proceedings, in which they argue unproductively, or in which they seem happy to go along with whatever anyone says without any reflection or debate. So there is an apparent paradox: teachers are able to specify what makes a good discussion, but such discussions occur very rarely in classrooms. Why should this be so?

One likely reason is that we may too readily assume that most children know how to talk and work together, when asked to do so, and so we rarely give explicit guidance or training in how to make a good discussion happen. We rely on children's wider social language experience to provide them with the resources for thinking together, but that experience may not include enough reasoned discussion. Children may not be familiar with the communicative strategies involved, and talk is such a taken-for-granted aspect of life that people rarely reflect on how they use it. This is why it is crucial that teachers help children to understand speaking and listening, and to develop their repertoire of ways of using talk to get things done.

Activities 1–9 can be used in two ways:

- *before* deciding on ground rules for talk to ensure that everyone has the necessary experience of collaborative group work;
- *after* creating the class ground rules, to reinforce particular skills and to ensure that the rules are doing what they should – making sure groups ask everyone to join in, ask for and provide reasons, negotiate ideas and try to come to an agreement.

Notes on teaching Thinking Together

- **It is essential to establish a shared set of ground rules for exploratory talk:**

  - Learning intentions for speaking and listening should be shared with the children and discussed in the closing plenary.

  - Activities suggested need to be straightforward because what is actually being learned are the more difficult skills needed to discuss things effectively with others.

  - Activities can be used with your own contexts for talk.

  - Practise a 'Please stop talking' signal before group work. During group work you can visit groups or send a child round to tell everyone to expect the stop signal soon.

  - Ensure that you feel confident to have children talking in situations where other classes are quiet. This means being able to explain your rationale in terms of speaking and listening for thinking and learning. You may need to be 'on a mission' with this. In some schools such work is usual; in others, it is highly unusual. Exploratory talk in your classroom should not be misunderstood as inappropriate behaviour.

- **Do we really need another set of classroom rules?** Yes. Each child has their own deep understanding of 'rules' that they have learned to govern their talk with others. This range of contradictory and unhelpful rules is what creates problems such as dominance, lack of reasoning and disrespect. A class must create its own *explicit* ground rules for talk that everyone has agreed to use.

- **Should we really be teaching children ways to talk to one another?** Yes. Although well equipped with their own spoken language, children benefit from being taught other ways to talk; Thinking Together is a powerful social and educational set of language tools. Far from supplanting or replacing what the child already knows, Thinking Together lessons simply offer them another string to their bow – a voice in the classroom.

About grouping

- Groups of three, boys and girls, helps to ensure a range of opinions.

- Mixed ability groups ensure that each group has a reader if needed.

- Friendship groups are not helpful because friends may agree too readily to generate discussion and are also very good at distracting one another.

- Each child should know that they have been allocated to a particular group for a positive reason, e.g. they are: good at general knowledge; co-operative; creative; a good listener; good at thinking up questions; a good reader; supportive of others; friendly; good at asking probing questions.

- Groups should remain together for several activities if possible. Problems – and there will be some – should be discussed by the whole class and suggestions offered. Ultimately, it should be possible to ask any children from the class to form a group.

- Children with extreme behaviour problems can, if it helps them, work with a different group for each session. As a 'guest' they benefit from the opportunity to listen to a range of models of good discussion. They can be asked to contribute examples of effective talk in the plenary, and the group can provide positive feedback of their guest's positive moves towards achieving the learning intentions. This strategy is successful if a supporting adult also moves with the child until they understand how the system works; the adult then gradually withdraws.

- Seating arrangements make a surprising difference; make sure children know that. Sitting around the end of a table works well.

- If the children are sharing a paper resource, pencil, scissors, the mouse – anything at all – then how it is shared should be discussed in advance to avoid ownership and distracting disputes.

- Ensure that all children are asked to take a turn reporting on their group's discussion.

- Move around the groups, listening, re-focusing, suggesting and questioning – that is, offering a model for how discussions are conducted. As children gain an understanding of how to think together, you can withdraw this support, telling the children why you are able to let them carry on alone.

Exploratory talk

Thinking Together activities encourage children to use 'exploratory talk'.

Exploratory talk is talk in which everyone is invited to give their ideas. Children know how to challenge one another respectfully, share information, and give and ask for reasons. Contributions may be hesitant first attempts to articulate new thinking. There is active listening and interest in different points of view. Children know that it is a strength to change their mind in response to a good reason or line of thinking. Group discussion proceeds as everyone seeks to reach an agreement.

> Talk is the most important way of working on understanding. Talk is flexible: in talk [children] can try out new ways of thinking and reshape an idea in mid-sentence, respond immediately to the hints and doubts of others, and collaborate in shaping meanings they could not hope to reach alone. The support of other members of the group is important, as is the need to reshape one's own ideas to incorporate their diverse ideas. [. . .] Small group talk encourages exploration of ideas, rather than presentation of certainties. [. . .] Exploratory talk is more likely in a small group of peers partly because the price of failure is lower: even twenty boys and girls can seem a threatening audience when one is uncertain. Members of a small group can risk hesitation and confusion, changes of direction, and rejection of their ideas by the others. The hesitancy and flexibility of exploratory talk is potentially a strength when students are talking in order to reshape and reinterpret ideas.
>
> (Barnes & Todd 1995: 15)

> Exploratory talk represents a joint, co-ordinated form of co-reasoning in language, with speakers sharing knowledge, challenging ideas, evaluating evidence and considering options in a reasoned and equitable way. The children present their ideas as clearly and as explicitly as necessary for them to become shared and jointly analysed and evaluated. Possible explanations are compared and joint decisions reached. By incorporating both constructive conflict and the open sharing of ideas, exploratory talk constitutes the more visible pursuit of rational consensus through conversation. Exploratory talk foregrounds reasoning. Its ground rules require that the views of all participants are sought and considered, that proposals are explicitly stated and evaluated, and that explicit agreement precedes decisions and actions. It is aimed at the achievement of consensus. Exploratory talk, by incorporating both conflicting perspectives and the open sharing of ideas represents the more visible pursuit of rational consensus through conversations. It is a speech situation in which everyone is free to express their views and in which the most reasonable views gain acceptance.
>
> (Mercer & Littleton 2007: 62)

THINKING TOGETHER ACTIVITIES

Activity 1: Talk works

Learning intention
To understand the purpose of speaking and listening.

- Think aloud with your class about the *jobs* that people can get done through talk.

- What do the children suggest when asked for their ideas?

By talking with others, people can:

- explain
- question
- remember
- solve puzzles and problems
- decide things
- make things up

- tell people how they feel
- find out how others feel
- justify a point of view
- inform
- discover
- share knowledge and information.

Ask your class to provide examples of these types of 'talk work'. Point out *what sort* of talk is happening during the whole-class work; introduce the idea of 'a good discussion' as a special sort of talk, focused on the task in hand, in which everyone works to support one another and further each other's understanding. Help children to see that taking part in such talk is why they are in class.

Activity 2: What's important about talk?

Learning intention
To understand the importance of speaking and listening.

Ask the whole class, or groups, what they think about these questions:

- How did you learn to talk? Who taught you? How did they do that?

- Have you helped to teach anyone else how to talk?

- How many languages can you speak?

- Who do you like to talk to, at home, in the playground, in class? What is good about it?

- What sort of things do we get done through talking together?

- When is it difficult to talk to people?

- What can go wrong if you don't get to talk to people?

- Are there times when you are asked not to talk? How do you feel then?

- What do you do to start a conversation with someone new?

- What do you do to end a conversation you are not enjoying?

- Which do you prefer, phone or email? Why?

- Can you think of a favourite word or phrase that you use? That another person uses?

- Who makes you laugh by talking? How do they do that?

- Why do we ask you to be quiet in class?

- When is it helpful to have someone to talk to in class? Who helps you this way?

- What sorts of things can you say that will help other people in our class?

- Do you think people should help each other? Is it cheating if they do?

Bring out the ideas that by working together, everyone does better than each person would alone; that everyone in class is a good resource for everyone else; and that explaining and describing things helps you to sort out and make sense of your own ideas.

Establish the idea that talk is a valuable tool for thinking together and getting things done.

Activity 3: Collective remembering

Outline

Children listen and recall, using what James Wertsch, Professor of Education at Washington University, St Louis calls 'collective remembering' (Wertsch 2002). Memory of an activity can be thought of as being *distributed* around the class as they listen to a text together, then try to piece it together afterwards. By talking about what we recall, we lay out our memories for comparison, confirmation and correction, building up a joint picture of things past. Of course, memory can be stimulated by taste, touch, sounds, sights and scents as well as by speaking and listening. We commonly use collective remembering to help children recall key features of previous lessons, or what they experienced on a school trip. They should be aware that this is a powerful tool for learning. What is recalled inevitably has an individual perspective or is represented in a particular way. Knowing this and what it means to offer a clear description can help children in and out of class – for example, when talking to you and others about playground problems. In this activity, speaking and listening together calls up the details that help the class to re-create what they know and understand.

Learning intention

To know that we can listen and remember to help us learn.

Explain the learning intention. Remind children that active listening involves thinking. Ask them to try to imagine pictures as you read a description.

Read **Parry's Journey** or another suitable text.

Parry's Journey

Parry shook his bike and jumped on as it moved. He had to get to the park. Because it was so cold, the handlebars felt hard to grip and the gear change was stiff. There was no wind but going fast down hill made the air rush by.

It was so early that he only saw one car moving, and that was an old taxi going in the opposite direction, its engine noisy and its lights glaring. All the other cars were still as if set solid by the frost. Parry's jacket was thin and unzipped and his chilly fingers began to feel as if they were being bitten. He braked to turn on to the canal bridge. The wheel rims sent out a raw squawk, very loud in the silence.

Crossing the canal, there was yellow light from a boat in a circle on the water, and a thin grey mist that wasn't moving. The water birds were all on the towpath, each a little huddle like a warm stone. Parry stayed on the road, trying to keep his weight balanced over the handlebars to get the front wheel to grip. Somewhere a church bell rang. A dog began to bark. An engine started, and the railings along the park appeared in a stiff row.

He reached the park gates and stopped suddenly, his breath in a cloud around him. What if –

Group work

Ask the children to talk together to:

• Say what they heard.

• Make up three questions that will check memories of the description. They should be able to answer the questions themselves. An example might be 'What sound did Parry hear after crossing the canal?'

• Put their question to another group.

• Add an ending or a further few sentences to the description.

• Analyse their talk, thinking about shared memory. How can people help one another by reminding and recalling? Illustrate this by recreating, as a class, a shared memory, e.g. of an assembly, a school journey, a previous lesson. Make the link between talk, thinking and recall explicit and, if appropriate, introduce and describe the idea of collective remembering. When is it useful?

• Think of some key phrases that will remind one another to use shared memory: 'Do you remember . . . ?', 'What about when we . . . ?', 'Can you remind me . . . ?', and so on.

Activity 4: Completing activities together through discussion

Outline
In groups, children discuss choices and make a reasoned selection of resources to create a joint picture. Within the group there are different tasks to do that contribute to the finished work. Essentially, the children undertake a simple open-ended activity that requires them to use the difficult skills of negotiation through talk, with a focus on encouraging respect for the choices of others.

Resources

– Use **5.1 Choose-it!** and **5.2 Word list** (one of each per group).

– Also:

  • scissors
  • glue
  • highlighter pens
  • felt tips
  • stencils
  • collage materials
  • coloured A4 paper.

- Red, blue and green tables with words, information and equipment as detailed on **5.3 Resources on the colour tables**.

• **'Here's one I made earlier'** picture if needed for demonstration.

Introduction

Learning intention
To use talk to share ideas and make a decision.

Explain the learning intention, and that the groups are going to think about words that seem to go together. The group's ideas are going to be used to make a picture. Each group's picture will be very different. The overall aim of this activity is for children to support all members of their group, respect one another's ideas, and come to joint decisions. They must collaborate using talk in order to achieve a satisfactory outcome.

Group work
Share learning intentions for speaking and listening to do with respect for one another's ideas. Discuss talk structures that enable collaboration:

- Shall we . . . ?

- Would you like to . . . ?

- What do you think . . . ?

- I agree because . . .

- I disagree because . . .

Make clear the idea that such collaborative talk is the focus for the lesson, and that you would like children to be aware of this so that everyone can contribute examples of such talk to the plenary session. Individual children must choose a colour (red, blue or green) so that they can collect equipment, words and information you have set out on the colour tables.

Provide each group with **5.1 Choose-it!** and **5.2 Word list**. Listen to group talk as the children work, collecting examples of high quality collaborative talk and reasoning. Timing depends on how well the class collaborates. You may wish to have a mini-plenary to re-state the lesson aims or share examples of effective talk.

Whole-class plenary
Can groups offer examples of 'a good discussion'? What negotiation was required? Can children provide examples of talk that showed respect for others, or in which someone changed their mind, or was persuaded by a good reason? Who was good at sharing information? At talking about choices? Giving ideas and suggestions? Listening?

5.1 Choose-it!

1   Talking and thinking together is very important in this lesson.

2   Start by reading out loud *all* the words on **5.2 Word list**.

3   Now talk together, discussing ideas by:

- listening carefully
- making sure that you try to understand everyone's point of view.

Choose:

(a)   1 word from box A
(b)   3 words from box B
(c)   6 words from box C

For now, you can only have TEN words altogether.

Decide on the reasons why you have chosen the words.

Make sure you all agree on your group's words.

4   Your group is now going to make a picture using your words.

5   You need some equipment and information.

One person at a time can now leave the table.

You can only go to the table of your colour – red, green or blue – to:

(a)   collect equipment
(b)   collect information
(c)   swap a word for one of the new words on the table

Remember:

- ONE person at a time can go.
- They can only collect or swap ONE thing at once!

You can ask the group which words or equipment they think would be useful, once you have looked at what is on your colour table.

6   Arrange your words on your display page. Decide how to make them really stand out.

- Which words go together?
- Can you illustrate the words or arrange them in a pattern?
- How big will words be?
- What colours and shapes will you use and why?
- How will you make sure that the title word stands out?
- Where will you put your own names?

Use everyone's ideas to put your **Choose-it!** picture together.

5.2 Word list

Box A

> day night journey games stories
> music sing laugh friends meetings time
> people places party family talk

Box B

> film computer mouse rainy
> play indoors jump smile shout cold
> game theme park dark light noise snow run
> grass colour sleep moon sea race desert
> dream shiny fast hot dog seaside
> travel learn think book bat
> cat hat ill activity

Box C

> badge ticket tired train grey
> red blue bike sunny earth scared
> car stars excited talk caravan dragon think
> play tent rules walk swim boat run den
> home sand castle lake mountain eat
> plane key space watch empty alone
> crowded funny gold big
> old mystery dance

5.3 Resources on the colour tables

RED TABLE

- Scissors/highlighters/pictures of items in the word list/collage material
- Plane shapes to draw round

Swap words: magic   outside   win   share

Information

- Your group can make up TWO extra words of your own.

- Decide how to arrange the words on your picture – what will you draw?

- The words don't have to be the same size or colour.

BLUE TABLE

- Glue/stencils/collage material

Swap words: prize   present   box   money

Information

- You can write the words or cut them out.

- You can stick the words down flat, fold them, bend them, zig-zag a piece of paper to hold them out – anything you like!

- Read out your words and arrange them so that they **sound** good.

GREEN TABLE

- Felt tips/coloured A3 paper/collage material

Swap words: silver   help   danger   forest

Information

- The word in Word List box 1 is the TITLE of your picture.

- Perhaps you can make flaps to cover some words.

- Make sure your group's names are on your picture.

Ask each group in turn to show and explain their picture. Encourage others to ask questions. Why were certain words chosen? What was the thinking behind the layout of the picture? Enable groups to provide feedback for one another. Ask children to leave their places to look at and think about one another's work. Provide sticky notes on which children can leave a positive comment.

Finally, ask groups to discuss their ideas for titles of future Choose-it pictures.

Extension

1   For children who speak another language, ask the child, parent or TA to translate words into home languages or make a bilingual picture.

2   Ask each group to write a brief paragraph explaining their choices, giving reasons. Display pictures with this paragraph. Ask each group to draw a small picture of themselves and add to the display. Each person should be drawn with a speech bubble, agreed by the group, which might say something like:

> I am good at listening/talking/asking questions/giving reasons/sharing information/helping others/working in a group.

3   Once they are familiar with the materials, children might benefit from the chance to re-group and repeat the Choose-it activity, discussing in advance what groups of words they intend to choose and why.

4   Theme picture. Use the Choose-it structure, for example, to do the following: categorise materials or creatures in science; to introduce a new story or geography topic; or, in art, to bring out learning about colour, shape or texture words.

Activity 5: What's a good discussion?

Provide each group with a dictionary and thesaurus.

Group work 1
Ask children to think together to make up a list of five statements describing what they understand by the phrase 'a good discussion'. Offer this phrase in context, for example 'I would like you to have a good discussion about your five statements!'.

Children can take roles for this activity, acting as scribe, researcher, reporter, and so on. These roles should be discussed and decided before the talk activity is described. Ask the children to use the talk tools 'I agree because . . .' and 'I disagree because . . .'.

Take ideas from one group at a time, ensuring all groups contribute. Highlight duplications that indicate class agreement.

Keep a note of ideas or collect the children's written ideas.

5.4 About exploratory talk

What is it?

A sort of talk that has been found to help everyone learn together.

What does it sound like?

- Everyone listens and joins in, talking clearly and with respect.

- Anyone can challenge or agree, as long as they give reasons.

- Everyone does their best to share new ideas and information.

Which words might we hear in exploratory talk?

I think . . . because . . . I agree because . . . I disagree because . . . why . . . but . . . what if . . . I remember . . . can you tell us . . . could you say a bit more about . . . my idea is . . . I have changed my mind because . . . that is a good point . . . in my opinion . . .

Why should we use exploratory talk?

To make clear what you know and understand at the moment. Then you can go on to learn more. Also, to help others in your group learn more.

What learning happens during exploratory talk?

Everyone shares what they think, so everyone can learn from one another. Talking helps people to make sense of new ideas and new experiences.

You can try out ideas by putting thoughts into words for others to hear and talk about.

Group work 2

Learning intention
To know what exploratory talk is, and why and how to use it.

Provide each group with a copy of **5.4 About exploratory talk**. Explain the learning intention and that exploratory talk is a special kind of talk that people use for discussion. Ask children to read the questions and ideas, and then think together by discussing:

- their own ideas about talk, in comparison with those given;

- the reasons for any differences;

- the advantages of exploratory talk;

- what makes it difficult to have a discussion using exploratory talk.

Activity 6: What do you think and why do you think that?

- Remind the children of the importance of exploratory talk for thinking and learning.

- Provide each group with a copy of **5.5 A trip to the shop**. Read the story aloud.

- Ask groups to think together using 'What do you think?' and 'Why do you think that?'. Stress the importance of asking for and giving *reasons* to come to decisions about the Talking Points. After discussion, ask the groups to give their ideas with reasons. Ask for different points of view and relate them to one another.

- Ask the groups to give examples of exploratory talk or examples of questions and reasons. Ask for suggestions of who listened carefully, asked questions, gave reasons, or was supportive in keeping the discussion going.

- Ask the groups to write a story ending and act it out for the class, or to draw a cartoon ending with speech bubbles for display. Discuss the children's ideas about the issues raised in the story.

Activity 7: Coming to an agreement

Christine Howe, Professor of Education at Cambridge University, carried out detailed research on children working in groups to complete science tasks (Howe 2003). An interesting finding was that learning was influenced by asking groups to discuss their ideas and reach agreement, or *consensus*, before carrying out their science investigation. It seemed to help learning just to try to reach agreement, even if this wasn't achieved. Having discussed ideas and made joint decisions, children are better prepared for guidance from their teacher, which is then both manageable and meaningful to them. The group's decision may reflect genuine agreement or be less firmly held; but the process of agreeing a course of action or a hypothesis may help the group to keep their

5.5 A trip to the shop

Sam was allowed to take Poppy to the shop now, strapped into her pushchair. Poppy was only two. The shop was five minutes walk and there was a pelican crossing, but it was still a big responsibility. Sam felt quite proud as they strolled along, with Poppy chattering away and hugging her toy tiger. At the shop, she chose a lolly and Sam had a chocolate cone. Sam sat on the wall outside to unwrap them. Poppy licked hers happily. It began to melt and run over her fingers.

That's when things started to go wrong.

Suddenly Alex appeared round the corner, coming towards them. Alex was smiling, nastily. Sam kept out of Alex's way at school. Alex was usually in a big gang who seemed to get each other into trouble or just to fight among themselves.

'Nice ice cream, Sammy!' said Alex, standing right in front of Poppy's pushchair. 'You can go and get me one.'

'But I don't have any money,' said Sam.

'Nor do I,' said Alex. 'No problem. Just go in and take one.'

'Here – have mine,' said Sam, holding out the cone. 'I haven't started it.'

Alex knocked it to the ground and stamped on it, then started kicking the pushchair wheels. Poppy squawked and looked frantically at Sam.

'Go on. Run in and get one. I'll look after the pushchair. Or maybe hers will fall on the floor as well . . .' Alex reached out to grab Poppy's lolly. She screeched and snatched it away, and now Alex, sneering, grabbed the toy tiger and held it up in the air. Poppy wailed.

'Yeah . . . or this might fly on to the road . . . go on Sammy, I want a choc ice, NOW . . .'

Talking Points: A trip to the shop

Talk together using exploratory talk. Make sure that everyone is asked 'what do you think?' and 'why?' to find out reasons.

- Sam and Alex are both boys – or are they girls . . .?

- Alex does not really want an ice cream.

- Alex is an unbelievable character.

- Losing the toy tiger is not important compared to committing the crime of shoplifting.

- Sam would act differently if Poppy were not there.

- There are ways to deal with bullies that stop them doing it.

- Sam has many choices at the end of the story – we can say what they are.

focus and make progress in their thinking. Children 'stimulated by consensus' (Howe & Tolmie 2003: 64) may be better able to refer to their agreed hypothesis or course of action as they proceed through the activity. They have talked and thought about their ideas, and have this as a resource to draw on, so each child avoids the worry that they are alone in their thinking. Consensus offers groups the chance to clear the decks and get going on a common idea. If it proves to be 'wrong' in some way, the safety-net of the group is there to prevent any one individual losing too much confidence. It's very stimulating to be part of a group that makes a discovery and generates new learning for everyone.

Outline. Children work in groups to think about their break times in school. They find out what others think about break times by conducting some classroom research.

- Ask the groups to think together to discuss **5.6 Break research**. Stress the importance of reaching a consensus. Once agreement is reached, groups make *brief* notes of their ideas for others to read.

- Ask groups to think up further Talking Points. Pair up with a different group to discuss the new Talking Points, again reaching agreement and noting key ideas.

- Each group now takes a separate Talking Point. Everyone gives their notes and ideas to this presenting group. Ask groups to present ideas in a lively, meaningful way with everyone taking part. Discuss ideas; what changes could be made to break time?

- Talk about the information that has been shared and the quality of the group discussion. What makes it easier to talk with others? Bring out the importance of listening and explaining clearly, as well as highlighting previous learning such as showing respect for other points of view. Check that children feel they have achieved the learning intentions

Extension

Pairs or groups can interview children from other classes during lessons or at break time.

Discuss other issues: homework; the curriculum; marking; what will happen at Parent's Evening; school uniform; assembly; use of the school grounds; evaluation of initiatives such as reading buddies; a new timetable.

5.6 Break research

Talk together to decide on your ideas, opinions and reasons.

Write your ideas briefly and neatly for other groups to use.

Record ideas as:

  – **yes, because . . . ;**

  – **no, because . . . ;**

  – **unsure, because . . .**

1 We usually enjoy break time.

2 Break time is too short.

3 Lunch time is too short.

4 School meals/packed lunches are good for us and nice to eat.

5 It is easy to relax and have a talk to people at lunch time.

6 There should be more things to play with outside.

7 We should be able to stay inside if we want to.

8 Some people take over the playground.

9 Sometimes it would be more interesting to carry on with class work.

10 At break we talk about what we have done in class.

11 We know who to go to if we need help.

12 We only play with people in our class.

13 The playground is an interesting place to be.

14 It would be better at break if . . .

Now think together to make up your own talking points.

Discuss them, then choose a different group and discuss the talking points with them.

Can you come to an agreement?

Activity 8: Challenges!

Outline
Groups discuss climate change using a jigsaw strategy.

In advance
Collect or bookmark a range of information resources about climate change. Organise your class into groups of four.

Learning intention
To be able to ask for and give reasons for ideas.

Explain the learning intention. Ask the groups you have established to *separate* so that each person works in one of four *research groups*. Use **5.7 Climate change**, divided into its four sections, one per research group.

Group work 1
Ask the *research* groups to discuss the issues. Children should not make notes unless you have a particular reason for wishing them to do so. If they are asked to write, the discussion will be much less effective. They should be made aware that for this activity, their memory will be the best way to retain information. Timing depends on the class but allow about 15 minutes. Once research time is complete, ask the original groups to reconvene.

Group work 2

–   Use **5.8 Talking Points: Climate change ideas**.

–   Ask the groups to read the instructions, then discuss everyone's ideas, making sure that they use key talk tools:

- – What do you think?
- – Why?
- – I agree because . . .
- – I disagree because . . .
- – My opinion is . . .
- – I have found out that . . .
- – My reason is . . .
- – But . . .

After discussion, organise a plenary in which:

•   Dialogue between yourself and the children enables ideas to be aired and suggestions heard.

•   The class evaluates the quality of their group talk, with a focus on identifying others who challenged and listened in a courteous manner.

97

5.7 Climate change

Using cars

Car engines burn petrol. This fuel is made from the remains of plants stored in the earth for thousands of years. Burning petrol releases carbon dioxide into the air. Carbon dioxide is an invisible gas that occurs naturally. It is necessary for life because plants use it to make sugar in their leaves. Too much carbon dioxide traps too much of the sun's warmth into the earth's atmosphere. This is global warming and it causes very extreme sorts of weather like floods and storms.

This effect is called climate change. There are now so many cars that we are noticing climate change. People drive instead of walking. People expect to have at least one car for every family.

Maybe we could walk, cycle or use public transport more?

Electricity

We use electricity to power many machines and to light our homes.

Electricity is generated in power stations by burning coal, oil or gas.

This burning sends the invisible gas, carbon dioxide, into the air.

Carbon dioxide occurs naturally too.

Its effect is to help trap the warmth from the sun, keeping earth warm enough for us to live.

But EXCESS carbon dioxide traps too much warmth.

Warmth melts the polar ice caps.

Wildlife is damaged.

Flooding is caused.

Extreme storms, heat and drought mean that people are in danger.

Maybe we should use less electricity?

Greenhouse gases

In the last 200 years, the amount of carbon dioxide in the atmosphere – the major gas that causes climate change – has increased by 30 per cent.

Greenhouse gases include carbon dioxide and carbon monoxide. Both occur naturally.

The greenhouse effect means that some gases in the air trap warmth from the sun into the atmosphere. This warmth is essential for life on earth. Too much carbon dioxide traps too much heat; the problem is that excess global warming causes climate change.

Concentrations of greenhouse gases are now higher than at any point in the past 800,000 years.

Perhaps we ought to think about how to reduce the amount of greenhouse gases we make?

Climate change myths

1 *Climate change will make the UK warmer so it will be more pleasant to live here*: it may be warmer, but there will be more floods and storms, and our wildlife will be damaged. Sea level rise will mean loss of land near the coast.

2 *It is too late to do anything about it*: no, not yet. Every time that less electricity or petrol is used, less carbon dioxide goes into the air, and this means there is less risk of excess global warming for people in the future.

3 *I can't do anything anyway*: everyone on earth can take responsibility for how much carbon dioxide they cause to be put into the atmosphere.

Perhaps we ought to think about what taking responsibility means?

5.8 Talking Points: Climate change ideas

- Read each talking point aloud, then discuss it with your group.

- Remember that the quality of your talk is extremely important.

- Use these words to express your ideas:
    - What do you think . . .?
    - Why . . .?
    - I agree because . . .
    - I disagree because . . .
    - My opinion is . . .
    - My reason is . . .
    - I have found out that . . .
    - But . . .

Try to keep in your mind a good example of any of these words in use, so that you can share it with everyone during the plenary.

Talking Points: Do you agree or disagree with one another?

1   The greenhouse effect is a bad thing for the planet.

2   Climate change is caused by people.

3   Carbon dioxide is a chemical that does not occur in nature.

4   All of us are responsible for putting carbon dioxide into the air.

5   Leaving the television on standby causes climate change.

6   It is too late to do anything about global warming.

7   Global warming doesn't matter; it will just make it warmer and that will mean we have better summers.

8   Global warming is the fault of car drivers.

9   We can think of ways that we could make a difference to how much carbon dioxide goes into the air.

10   If the polar ice cap melts, we will have no polar bears on earth. That doesn't matter because we never see them anyway.

Now decide together how to draw a diagram to illustrate how carbon dioxide causes global warming.

- Discuss reasoning, its importance, and how it's possible to tell what is a good reason or a poor reason.

- Discuss problems groups may have had, with the class suggesting strategies to help.

Extension

Ask groups to create a PowerPoint presentation to highlight their ideas and what points were dilemmas. Share with the class.

Ask groups to choose one of the four areas, or a different topic (wildlife, the polar ice caps, catastrophic weather events, energy in the home; our food, and so on) to prepare material to create an interactive display that will stimulate further discussion.

Activity 9: Elaborate!

Outline

Children play a simple dice game called 'Elaborate!'. The example included here has a science content, but Elaborate! cards can be created for any curriculum area. Cards are set out in a circle, face up. The children take turns to throw the dice. The number shown dictates both how far the child's counter travels, and the talk task the child is asked to do once they land on a card. Children practise group talk skills but especially the capacity to elaborate. The aim of the game is to use one another's support to gain confidence in talking about the topics on the cards. After the group work, each group is asked to select one topic to explain to the class, answering questions – that is, to *elaborate* their understanding.

Resources

Every group needs:

- One set of cards
- A dice
- A pair of scissors
- Coloured counters
- Paper and pencils
- *Optional*: electronic or text research resources.

Introduction

Learning intention
To understand how to elaborate, explain or add detail.

Explain the learning intention, and define the word *elaborate* as *adding detail* or *explaining further* (or ask the children to find in a dictionary and note its alternative but related use, to *complicate*). Ask the children to reflect on and share what might be the advantages of elaborating ideas in group work. Bring out the idea that, as people talk, they put into words thoughts that may not have been clear before; they draw on all they know to inform what they say. By elaborating we can help ourselves, and others, understand. Discussion is closed down by brief, laconic or throw-away responses. There are ways that we can help others to say more or elaborate.

In educationally effective group work, elaboration must be relevant to the topic.

Display these talk tools that help people to elaborate, and ask for examples of use:

- Can you say more about . . . ?

- Can you explain again . . . ?

- What do you mean by . . . ?

- How do you know about . . . ?

- What you said about . . . was interesting – can you add detail . . . ?

Using **5.9 Elaborate!** explain the *aims* of the game and prepare the children for their role in the plenary. Ensure that they understand how, and why, they will be playing this game. Stress taking turns; collaboration; using prompts to encourage one another; and mention that the ultimate success is for groups to remember to talk like this when they are not playing a game.

Using the dice, go through the numbers on the dice, modelling each type of talk and checking for understanding:

1 make up a sentence

2 definition

3 spelling

4 paraphrase

5 question

6 elaborate.

Example: Throwing a dice and moving the counter to the *Light* card:

1   Use the words on the card to think of a sentence about the topic.

   Shadows are formed when opaque objects block light.

2   Choose a word from the card and describe or define what it means.

   Vision means the ability to see with our eyes.

3   *Spelling*: A group mate takes the card and the child is asked to spell a word from it.

   e.g. *reflection*

4   *Paraphrase*: A child uses the word on the card to think of a sentence. Group mates paraphrase this – that is, put it in their own words, using 'so you are saying that . . .', or 'in other words . . .'.

   Child: *Reflection is when light bounces off something.*

   Paraphrase: *In other words, light hits something and is reflected back.*

5   *Question*: A child thinks of a question about the topic to ask group mates. They may be able to answer it themselves, or not. Reference books and the internet can be used to answer questions if children wish to do this. Questions are recorded for use in the plenary.

   How far is a light year?

   A light year measures the distance between stars and is the distance that light will travel in a year. The speed of light is 186,000 miles per second. A light year is about 6 million million miles.

6   *Elaborate*: A child prepares, then is timed for one minute talking about the topic. Group mates support by using talk tools.

   Variation: After thirty seconds the child can 'PASS' the topic to a group mate to continue. *Times* can be altered to suit your class, building up to one minute.

Group work
With children in groups of three or four, provide **5.9 Rules for Elaborate!** and **5.10 Elaborate! Cards**. Allow about twenty minutes.

Whole-class plenary
Ask groups to choose a card and prepare to talk. If two groups choose the same card, both throw a dice and the lower number must choose a different card. Every child must contribute.

5.9 Rules for Elaborate! Dice game

Cut out the cards.

Arrange them face up in a circle.

Choose a counter each and put them on any card.

Everyone throws the dice; highest number starts.

First person throws the dice and counts clockwise round the cards.

If you throw a:

1. Use the words on the card to **think of a sentence** about the topic.

2. Choose a word from the card and **say what it means**.

3. *Spelling*. A group mate will ask you to spell a word from the card. Keep trying till you get one right! Replace the card.

4. Use the words on the card to think of a sentence.

   Your group mates now have to **paraphrase** what you've said – that is, put it in their own words, using *'So you are saying that . . .'*, or *'In other words . . .'*.

5. Think of a **question** about the topic and ask your group mates. Talk about or look up the answer. Write down your question and the answer.

6. **Elaborate!** Get ready! Read all the words on the card. Ask your group for help with meanings. Now you are going to talk about the topic for ONE MINUTE.

Group mates will help by using:

- Can you say more about . . . ?

- Could you explain again . . . ?

- What do you mean by . . . ?

- How do you know about . . . ?

- What you said about . . . was interesting – can you add detail . . . ?

Ready? Go!

Make a note of your **name** and the **topic** you have elaborated.

5.10 Elaborate! Science cards

Light	Materials	Nutrition
Sources; dark; reflection; shadow; speed; colour; vision	Properties; harness; strength; flexibility; absorbency	Food; growth; balanced diet; food groups; teeth; animals
Sound Sources; vibration; travels; pitch; volume; music; hearing	**Insulators** Warmth; metals; electricity; plastic; conductors	**Circulation** Heart; blood; veins; arteries; capillaries; lungs; oxygen
Electricity Circuit; battery; bulbs; series; parallel; wires; conductors	**Rocks and soils** Appearance: texture; permeability: colour; crystals	**Movement** Skeleton; bones; support; joints; muscles; tendons
Magnets North pole; south pole; attract; repel; magnetic field; compass; direction; electromagnet	**Changing materials** Heating; cooling; water; chocolate; ice; evaporation; condensation; non-reversible change	**Green plants** Light; water; temperature; growth; leaf; root; stem; germination; water; minerals
Force Push; pull; going faster; slowing down; changing direction; change shape; balanced forces	**Separating mixtures** Water; air; dissolve; solution; filter; evaporate; sand; sugar; crystals	**Variation** Keys; characteristics; insects; birds; people types; differences; similarities
Friction Grip; stopping; air resistance; water resistance	**Solid, liquid, gas** State; temperature; water; ice; steam; air; volume; flow	**Living things** Adapted; environment; food chains; micro-organisms

After the presentation, ask for questions on the topic with the whole class contributing to the answers.

Remind the class of the learning intention and ask for their opinions about whether they understand how to say more about what they know, taking turns and helping others take theirs. Ask the children to provide examples of effective group talk, especially elaboration.

Extension

Can the class suggest other topics for the game, or other rules to encourage further discussion?

Activity 10: Ground rules for exploratory talk

The most important section of this whole book!

Learning intention
To create and choose ground rules that will help everyone to use exploratory talk when working in a group.

Introduction: raising awareness of the importance of talk
Ask children for their ideas and opinions about:

- what makes a good discussion;
- why speaking and listening is important in a classroom;
- what they understand by the term 'exploratory talk' and why it is special;
- their understanding of the link between talk and thinking;
- how the class has a shared memory;
- sharing strategies for dealing with off-task talk;
- how they learn from one another through talk;
- someone who is a good listener and why.

Awareness of the value of shared ground rules for exploratory talk
Ask children to share their ideas about:

- what rules operate in the playground;
- what can happen if one or two people break the rules;

- what happens if a new child arrives who has in mind a different set of rules;

- the importance of shared rules.

Explain that the basic 'ground rules' for behaviour are often unspoken. Bring out the idea that we need to share rules for group talk, or things might go wrong – that is, special learning time will go to waste. Ask the children to give examples of ineffective group work – without naming others, what can be difficult or can stop learning?

Establish the idea that the class can create, share and agree on a set of ground rules for exploratory talk that will benefit everyone.

Creating and sharing ground rules for exploratory talk
Ensure that everyone knows the difference between 'important' and 'essential'.

– Use **5.11: Talking Points: Ground rules for exploratory talk**.

Group work 1
Ask the children to discuss the Talking Points. Listen to groups talking and note the points to be shared in whole-class work. You may wish to tackle the entire list or ask the children to concentrate on three or four talking points.

Organise a *mini-plenary* to share the issues raised.

Group work 2

– Use **5.12: Choosing ground rules for exploratory talk**.

Ask groups to think together to decide on a set of ideas or rules, which if used would help everyone to talk and think together. Establish the idea of positive language for rules, that is, it is best if the starter phrase 'Do not . . .' is avoided.

Whole-class plenary
Ask groups to explain their suggestions and comment on one another's ideas.

Tell the class that you will collect all suggestions and collate them to produce a set of ground rules for exploratory talk in the children's own words.

After the lesson

- Check that the class agrees with your summary.

- Ask the class if they can agree to use these rules to structure their discussions.

- If not, modify the rules.

- If the class agrees, they are then responsible for helping one another to stick to the rules; they should be able to give a reason for each rule and should know why the rules matter.

- Display the rules prominently.

- Provide individual copies for each child.

- Send a copy home to ask for comments.

- Ensure the rules are visible when children are working at computers together.

- Keep the rules in children's minds by mentioning in introductions, group work and plenaries. Focus on a particular rule if it is obvious that the class needs input.

- Ask children for examples of people who are using the rules during group talk.

- Share the rules with other classes/the school in assembly.

- Revise the rules if children feel that there is a problem with their discussion.

- Remind the children to use the rules and ask them to remind one another.

Examples of class ground rules for exploratory talk

Rules such as 'be polite', 'speak when you are spoken to' or 'always take turns' are social rules and inappropriate here. They will not help to generate a good discussion or exploratory talk. High quality talk in groups is characterised by being inclusive, on-task, and chained into lines of reasoning and coherence. An element of challenge is essential and the drive to seek an agreement useful.

Class ground rules are uniquely worded to embody the principles of exploratory talk. Two examples are:

Year Three's ground rules for exploratory talk

- Always include everyone.

- Share ideas with other people.

- Discuss things.

- Ask for opinions and reasons.

- We listen to others so we can learn.

5.11 Talking Points: Ground rules for exploratory talk

What does your group think about these ideas?

1   Talk and thinking are the same thing.

2   You are naturally good at talk or not, and nothing can be done about it.

3   Writing is more important than talk.

4   It is easier to talk well than it is to write well.

5   You can think without words.

6   'I talk when I think' is the same as 'I think when I talk'.

7   You can never tell what anyone else thinks.

8   It is rude to disagree with other people.

9   When other people talk, you can be thinking what you will say next.

10 It's impossible to tell if other people are listening.

11 Everyone can learn how to be part of a learning conversation.

12 Listening means being quiet.

13 If you ask questions it shows that you don't know anything.

14 Making mistakes when you talk to the whole class is not helping anyone.

15 People make fun of you if you let them know what you really think.

16 It is boring to talk about the things we learn in school.

17 We can explain what exploratory talk is and why it is important.

18 Quiet people are dull and can't help others learn.

19 Quiet people are lazy and have nothing to say.

20 Quiet people are thinking interesting things, but don't want us to know.

21 If you share what you know out loud, other people will do better than you.

22 If you tell people things, it's cheating.

23 It's dishonest to stop and consider others. Say what you think.

24 Some people have no opinions or ideas.

5.12 Choosing ground rules for exploratory talk

Our group names: _____

Our suggestions for rules to encourage exploratory talk

listening	
joining in	
respect	
agree or challenge	
sharing opinions and ideas	
things that we know	
making decisions	
concentrating	
– your ideas –	

- Now put a star by your top three ideas.

- Identify six key words: _____ _____

  _____ _____

  _____ _____

- What problems do people have when they work in groups?

  _____

  _____

  _____

Year Five's ground rules for talk

- We can help each other by talking.

- We will always share and use everyone's ideas.

- We will think together before we do things.

- Everyone will listen carefully.

- We will ask, '*What do you think?*' and '*Why do you think that?*'.

- If there are problems we will sort them out by talking.

Talk and the level of difficulty of activities

Manuel Fernandez (Sub-Coordinator for Research, UNESCO, Mexico) researched children's talk in the Thinking Together project. He studied groups of children working together to write stories, emails and non-fiction texts. The children had previously discussed and established ground rules for talk. One of his useful findings was that:

- When tasks were too easy for the group, little talk took place. Since every-one knew what to do and why, there was no need for discussion.

- When tasks were too difficult for the group, disputes and recriminations were a feature of the talk, as children attempted to shift the responsibility on to others.

- Tasks that offered an appropriate level of challenge generated exploratory talk.

Activity 11: The value of interthinking

Introduce children to another useful speaking and listening term: *interthinking*. They may be familiar with the words *interacting* or *interactivity,* to mean reciprocal action, or action between people, or people and software. Explain the Latin prefix 'inter-' (among, between); ask them to think what interthinking might be and what effects it might have. Spoken language makes interthinking an everyday possibility. Interestingly, spoken language can also be used to interfere with the process of interthinking so that classroom conversations become less than educationally effective. When talking together using explora-tory talk, we are not just interacting, we are interthinking. This is a powerful way to learn by sharing the resources of our minds.

> **Interthinking in class**
>
> The concept of **interthinking** is a way to describe and understand learning with others.
>
> **Interthinking is our use of spoken language to support:**
>
> - thinking together;
>
> - collectively making sense of experience and solving problems;
>
> - joint, co-ordinated intellectual activity;
>
> - the dynamic interaction of minds;
>
> - the essential, collective nature of human thinking.
>
> Language is a tool for interthinking that each child can learn to use effectively.
>
> (Adapted from Mercer, 2000)

Interthinking activity

Outline

Using higher order thinking skills *analysis* and *evaluation*, children discuss talk to identify the features of exploratory talk and decide whether inter-thinking is taking place. Such experience makes it more possible to recognise and take opportunities for interthinking during group work.

Resources

- Use **5.13: The Vikings** and **5.14: Interthinking** (one per group).

- *Optional*: pictures of Viking ships, helmets, shields, etc.

In advance

Choose nine extrovert children, good readers, or good actors to help with the starter activity. In advance of the lesson, provide them with **5.13: The Vikings**. Allocate each child a role to practise. They should aim to read rather than learn by heart.

Learning intention

To know how and why we use interthinking in group work.

Introduction

Explain the learning intention. Discuss Viking artefacts and explain that the class is going to watch three groups 'working at the computer' on a programme in which they are acting as Vikings. Ask the children to listen carefully to the *talk* of each group. Ask the Narrator to begin; watch the short plays.

Group work

Ask children to think together about the ways children speak and listen in **5.13: The Vikings** plays. What comments can they offer? Do they have personal experience of any of the three sorts of talk? Which sort of talk do they think will help the group to succeed best with the software? Which sort of talk involves everyone? What problems arise in each play and how are they dealt with? Is any interthinking happening?

Use **5.14: Interthinking**. Ask the groups to interthink to analyse the talk they have heard and complete the talk analysis table. Share the results and ideas with the class. Which sort of talk is exploratory talk? What are its features? Which questions help others to talk?

Extension

Ask groups to take on playing the roles of the children as in the Vikings plays. Ensure that there is an even mix of Viking Groups 1, 2 and 3. The children can change their character's name, add a character or change whether the children are boys or girls, but they cannot change the *way the children talk to each other*. Ask the groups to create a **One-minute play** in the speaking and listening style of their Viking group.

After the performance, ask the class to comment on how well the group have achieved the sort of talk they set out to create.

One-minute play!

- It is raining at break time and you all have to stay in.

- You can choose whether to play a board game, watch a DVD, or draw pictures.

- Each of you wants to do something different.

- Make up the conversation you have, remembering to decide on a good ending.

5.13 The Vikings

Narrator

The class were working at the computer. The children were acting as Viking invaders who had arrived on the coast in their long boats. They were looking for somewhere safe with water and food to go ashore and make camp.

We can listen to three groups making a decision about where to land and camp.

The first group is [*indicates*] Fenella and Germain.

Group 1 Fenella and Germain
[*Note to actors – this group is grumpy and loud!*]

F   OK – a place to land – let me see.

G   I know, I know, I'll show you.

F   You must be joking. You've had your go.

G   Well, I know where to land, go there, go there. [*tries to take the mouse*]

F   Oh, right, just where all the soldiers are waiting. [*clicks around, humming*]

G   For goodness sake, get on with it. Just go there then.

F   No.

G   Yes.

F   No. I know where to go. So just shut up and wait.

G   You don't know anything. I know where to go, I've done this screen once.

F   Rubbish. Anyway, hard luck, it's my turn. [*clicks again*]

G   The soldiers got you!! Ha ha! See! Told you it was wrong. Stupid. Right, my turn now. You'll see how to do it now. [*grabs the mouse*]

F   You wait. I bet you don't know where the treasure is. I do.

G   So you say. You are so useless at finding it, aren't you?

F   Only because you never let me have a go. Here – my turn. [*grabs the mouse*]

Narrator: Right. Very interesting. Thank you, Fenella and Germaine. Now we can look at Group 2 deciding where to land. Here are Pavel, Milly and Samra.

Group 2 Pavel, Milly and Samra
[*Note: this group is quiet and dull!*]

P   A place to land. Maybe there, by the church.

M   OK, whatever.

P   Or perhaps by that monastery. There might be treasure.

M   Oh, wow. Suits me.

P   Right, I'm landing by the monastery. Now, where should I camp . . .? By a stream . . .

M   By the stream, oh, yeah. Samra, are you having packed lunch today?

S   Yes.

P   Right, I am clicking on the stream for my camp. Oh no!! We have been flooded! We have lost all our horses!

M   You have, you mean. It's your fault; you chose the stream.

5.13 The Vikings *(continued)*

P   Quick, OK, I'd better get back to the boat.

M   OK. Whatever. Samra, can I borrow your pencil after break?

S   Yes.

P   Right, now. Try again. Where shall I camp? On the hill. [*clicks mouse*]

S   [*yawns*]

M   [*starts humming or singing a song, twiddling fingers, looking around*]

P   Oh, no. The soldiers have found my boat.

M   Good. We might as well pack up. [*yawns and stretches*]

Narrator [*yawning too*]: Is that it? Oh, well. Thank you very much Group 2. And now we can have a look at Group 3 choosing where to land. Here are Daren, Robyn and Alex.

Group 3 Daren, Robyn and Alex
[*Note: this group is friendly and enthusiastic!*]

D   We have to find somewhere to land, then make a camp.

R   What do you think?

D   I think, land by the church.

R   Why?

D   Um, because, it looks sheltered and we might not be seen.

R   Alex, what do you say? Land by the church?

A   I disagree because I don't know if those soldiers will stay asleep.

D   Oh, solidiers! I hadn't noticed them. You're right. Choose another place.

R   By the monastery.

A   Why?

R   There are cliffs and I don't think anyone would see the boats.

D   I'm not sure. Do you agree the monastery, Alex?

A   It's worth a try. Go on – click it, Daren. OK. Now, where should we camp? What do you think?

R   Um, by the stream because we need water.

D   By the stream. Yes. Why not? It looks flat there too. OK. We all agree. [*D clicks mouse*]

D   Oh, no!! 'There is a flood and you lose all your horses.'

A   We've lost our horses.

R   It's a disaster ! Hey, I know! Let's go back to the monastery and take some of theirs!

D   That's what Vikings would have done.

R   Yes, and move camp up on to the hill a bit, so it's not so wet.

A   Then we can leave some people cooking while we ride out and scout round the countryside.

R   Do you know where the treasure is, anyone?

A   Yes – you have to collect the key from the hut over by the wood, first.

D   OK. Right. Here we go!

5.14 Interthinking

Think together to analyse the children's talk in each of the Vikings plays.

Use the written copy of the plays to help you. Make sure you invite everyone to give their opinion and reasons, and that you reach agreement before putting a tick or cross.

The group in this play	Group 1 Fenella and Germain	Group 2 Pavel, Milly and Samra	Group 3 Daren, Robyn and Alex
Made sure that everyone contributed			
Asked each other questions			
Listened carefully to what was said			
Answered questions thoughtfully			
Gave reasons for ideas			
Shared everything they knew			
Were concentrating on the decisions they had to make			
Always agreed			
Made mistakes in the programme			
Sorted things out by agreeing a new plan			
All took responsibility for doing well or badly			
Respected one another's suggestions			
Are going to do well as Vikings			
Enjoyed working with one another			
Took plenty of time to talk things through before deciding			
Were interthinking			

Two more things to discuss:

• What difference does it make if the children are boys or girls?

• What difference does it make if there are two rather than three people in a group?

Summary

There is a close relationship between dialogic teaching and exploratory talk. Dialogic teaching involves creating the conditions in which children can express their ideas to an involved audience, elaborating areas of uncertainty and offering reasons for opinions. Coherence and meaning emerge from linked contributions. Exploratory talk does the same things, but happens between children in groups with no adult present. Dialogic teaching supports children in their learning of exploratory talk because it offers them a clear model for using talk for thinking collectively. The experience of being part of a whole class engaged in dialogue can help children to see that challenging others, expressing doubts, talking things through in detail and trying to keep on task have educationally powerful outcomes.

Exploratory talk is *symmetrical;* the participants are all equal in terms of status. This affects turn-taking and how outcomes are negotiated. Dialogic teaching is *asymmetrical* – the teacher has their hands on the reins. Who talks, the direction of the discussion and summing up are the teacher's responsibility. This is what teaching is; the professional expertise to create dialogue in which learning takes place. Exploratory talk, just as valuable for learning, is dependent on children's understanding of why and how they discuss things in groups. Many children need to be taught this. All will benefit from making explicit the hidden rules that muddle children and scupper their educational discussion. Whole classes can move forward by deciding which clear rules will really help them to talk and think together.

Learning through talk should not just be a chance occurrence, but an everyday event. Teaching Thinking Together – such as by using the activities in this chapter and indeed the entire book – offers a set of transferable skills and ensures that children have an understanding of the importance of their talk for learning. It is essential that teachers help to raise children's awareness of the speaking and listening tools that, once acquired, will benefit their thinking and learning over time and in any setting. The skills that contribute to the child's ability to take part in effective discussion are learnt in social settings. The classroom is, for all children, a crucial social context for learning how to learn through talk.

To become truly literate, children should be able to articulate their thoughts and ideas, challenge others and negotiate new understandings. If we limit our conception of literacy to reading and writing, and assume that talk skills will develop of their own accord, we miss essential opportunities to educate children. The Primary Framework's speaking and listening strands emphasise the importance of extending a child's repertoire of talk.

Lessons with learning intentions and plenary sessions that focus on talk and the chance to establish class *ground rules for talk*, enable children to think together using higher order thinking skills. Deep learning becomes possible. Evaluations of Thinking Together suggest that, by interthinking with one another, children internalise rational thought processes that help them to do better when working alone. Chances to reflect on how talk supports learning can give children insight into their own development and help them to see how they can positively influence others. There are social benefits as children learn how to give their own point of view, elicit and challenge the point of view of others with some respect, seek consensus and negotiate compromise.

It may take an entire school year for a class to be able to use exploratory talk independently of adult support. The increments of understanding are rather small and easily over-ridden by other models of speaking and listening behaviour. However, some children seem to 'catch on' to the idea from day one, finding their voice rapidly once offered the talk tools to do so. The powerful questions, 'What do you think?', 'Why?' come as a revelation to some children. They get to work on using them straight away. Their enthusiasm in using the class ground rules – ensuring that everyone contributes, requiring reasons for assertions, holding out for a negotiated consensus – is infectious and seems to raise the quality of discussion almost immediately. Once a critical mass is established, the whole class takes on the responsibility of making sure that they conduct 'a good discussion'.

The role of the teacher is to provide direct teaching of talk skills and to foster understanding of the relationship between speaking, listening, thinking and learning. In addition, the teacher offers a model of exploratory talk through dialogic teaching in whole-class settings. We can show that when problems are thoroughly discussed, joint decisions become possible. We can support children as they move into exploratory talk by keeping a focus on the talk itself as a learning outcome, and taking opportunities to remind children how often their discussion skills can be put to good use. Exploratory talk is tentative and hypothetical; teachers can value children's hesitant offerings and make sure that there is time to listen. Children can become active listeners for one another.

Thinking Together is a practical approach that can be integrated into planning across the curriculum. Strategies in this chapter's activities can be used for all curriculum areas. Children are motivated by the chance to discuss things during the lessons because they do like to talk to each other – and to us.

Further reading

Corden, R. (2000) *Literacy and Learning through Talk.* Buckingham: Open University Press.

Mercer, N. (2000) *Words and Minds.* London: Routledge.

CHAPTER 6

Speaking

Teaching children how to articulate their ideas

It seems important not to underrate children's language abilities. Faced with a full classroom, a topic they feel unsure about, and a teacher's questions that may conceal unforeseen implications, many children seem tongue-tied and incoherent, so that we value all the more those who can produce well-shaped replies. But this does not mean that the others cannot use language productively as a way of learning.

(Barnes 1992: 166)

From the moment I could speak I was ordered to listen.
(*Father and Son*; Cat Stevens)

Speaking usually needs someone to be listening. Children can provide one another with just the right audience, especially if they know what to listen out for – that is, if they understand how to evaluate what they hear and provide helpful feedback. By learning how to listen actively, children gain insight into their own capacity to act as a speaker. This can help increase confidence. Importantly, children can usefully begin to see that they can offer and receive constructive criticism.

Developing speaking skills

Children move from an informal approximation of what they hear – 'baby talk' – to a joining in with what their community says and how they say it. They learn to speak by copying others. Speaking aloud in school helps children to develop the skills and confidence they need to communicate in a range of contexts.

The progression in speaking skills is from talk with familiar adults or friends towards talk with strangers; and from reading or recounting known information to talking about their own ideas. Becoming articulate also involves

6.1 What speaking skills can we teach?

Speaking skill	Contexts	Progression
describe	events	audibly clearly
read aloud	given text own work	for meaning different ways variety of pace variety of emphasis
choral speaking	poem given text	clarity improved intonation
tell a story	given text own work oral story	including detail with props with expression use story language
explain	a process an idea	logically including detail
present information	from own research provided by others	logically including detail
perform	work of others own work	with meaning with expression volume and use of sound
sustain a conversation	about a given topic about ideas	elaborate take account of others
present a spoken argument	given topic personal topic	use reasons answer queries and points respect differences
ask and answer questions	questions devised in advance/with partner questions occur during talk	probing more thoughtful varied and sequenced
discuss ideas, topics, issues	partner group whole-class debate	increasing use of agreed ground rules
interview	friend other	devising questions responding to interviewee

Guest speaker: Prue Goodwin, Lecturer in Literacy and Children's Books, University of Reading

Pleasurable tales, powerful teaching

The blinds were drawn, the lights were off, a torch beam shone on the teacher's face as she started to speak: 'Once upon a time, on a dark and stormy night, I was walking home alone through the forest when I saw something strange on the ground. What on earth was it? I looked closely. It was a great, big, hairy TOE!'

The children stared open-mouthed, mesmerised. As the tale unfolded, the children gasped, shivered and squeaked with excitement as the monster got closer and closer and closer until . . . the unexpected climax left everyone giggling with relief.

An observer of this lesson may question various aspects of it. What planning had taken place? How well had the teacher presented the lesson? How would the learning outcome be assessed? But it could be argued that storytelling is something far more important than any curriculum requirement, and with a far greater potential for successful learning than any lesson plan. For a start, the children were totally engaged. If their teacher asked them to follow up the story with a retelling, drama or literacy activity, the expectation of enjoyment would motivate and sustain their 'work'. Importantly, there was now a model of how stories operate. Good stories – whether told or read aloud – can be vehicles for all sorts of learning, but if we want children to read and write stories themselves, they must have heard and told stories as often as possible.

Every day teachers tell and read stories from their cultural and literary heritage, but they also use narrative to explain practical ideas; for example, how water changes into ice; how two added to three makes five; what it was like to live in Victorian days. Even doing a forward roll in PE can be described as a narrative sequence – having an opening, a complication and a resolution. Provide a set of facts and they will soon be forgotten; put the same information into a story and it is easy to remember. Teaching involves using stories; narrative develops cognition, promotes abstract thought and offers that most powerful means of representing the world – metaphor.

In telling the monster story, the teacher was not only using a powerful tool for teaching, she was tapping into the natural inclination of all human beings to tell and listen to stories. Stories offer us order in a random universe and comfort in what can seem an irrational existence; they provide cognitive frames of reference through which we can make connections between ourselves, the physical world and the experiences of others. By telling, reading and listening to stories we learn what it is to be human. Stories are enjoyable, support learning, and most of all are an essential part of human experience. All classrooms should be full of stories.

progress from brevity, monosyllabic response or infantile approximations of words, to extended turns in conversations; and from saying what is immediately necessary to developing an awareness of the listener, asking and answering questions and reflecting on what will be said. Children who speak well can be expected to explore ideas with one another, sustaining the discussion by giving, listening to and reflecting on reasons, and to manage disagreement without this halting their interaction.

Whole-class talk sessions provide opportunities to help children move towards independence as speakers in a safe context. Whether a particular child speaks may depend on who else wishes to speak, how turns are organised, the child's perception of how others will respond and their confidence to join in. In turn, these factors depend on how you organise whole-class sessions. A child's contribution may also depend on how well they listen and think about what they are hearing. You can help children to understand these things and find their voice in the classroom.

Identified in **6.1 What speaking skills can we teach?** are some crucial speaking skills, a range of contexts and a progression that can be developed based on the 'Speaking' strand of the Primary National Strategy. Children can also learn to understand the criteria that are used to assess how they speak, but there is a fine line to tread between helping children to recognise and evaluate clarity of speech, and making them self-conscious and more likely to be tongue-tied. An overall learning intention is to enable children to communicate better through oral language.

An important aside: the quiet child

> Happy families are all alike; every unhappy family is
> unhappy in its own way.
>
> (Leo Tolstoy: *Anna Karenina*)

Noisy children seem all alike; every quiet child is quiet in their own way. Because quiet children are 'good' in class, they may escape notice. A thorough investigation of the underlying reasons for persistent quietness is the key to deciding whether or not to intervene. Children can be quiet in class because they are content, cowed or angry. They can refuse to speak if they perceive a threat or if something has happened to upset them, or if they need slightly longer to think. They may have hearing or language difficulties that affect their capacity to receive or process what they hear or see. They may just not feel like talking. Some children are habitually quiet; others never speak in school and become elective mutes. Some children are quiet in class much to the astonishment of their family on parents' evening, who report that they live with a chatterbox. Causes of quietness are extremely important, particularly psychological or medical causes, or causes related to a child's difficult relationships with their peers. We can ensure that every child is carefully attended to, properly assessed, and their difficulties addressed (see Further reading).

When devising activities with learning intentions for *speaking*, it is essential that there is a meaningful and important context. Your class topics, issues, stories, plays and poems will all provide contexts.

Thinking about speaking

Learning intention
To understand how talk works and what we can use it for.

Resources

— Use **6.2 Talk works**.

— *Or* collect photographs of people talking, from magazines, Oxfam web pages, or photographs provided by the children.

— Provide post-it notes.

Ask children to look at the pictures in pairs or a group.

Using class ground rules for talk, ask children to think together to decide:

- what the people are doing;

- what the people are saying;

- what they will do next because of what is said;

- a title for the picture.

Ask each group to write speech bubbles for the picture using post-its.

Complete this activity for two or three pictures, depending on time.

Now ask children to consider their ideas, and think together to decide what sorts of things we get done with other people through talk.

Ask groups to share their ideas with the class. Bring out examples such as: we give instructions how to do something, find a place if travelling, tell stories, read aloud, ask questions, give answers, share what we know, say what we have been doing or what we think, or ask for help. We listen to our friends.

6.2 Talk works

6.3 Talking Points: Speak up!

Read each Talking Point in turn.

Think together to agree on your group's ideas.

Make sure that *everyone* is invited to speak, using 'What do you think?' and 'Why do you think that?'

1 Talk is useful and we can think of lots of things you can do by talking.

2 It is difficult to speak sometimes and we can give examples.

3 Talk in class is different from talk at home.

4 There are lots of times when we are asked not to speak.

5 We can think of some people who are good speakers and say why.

6 We can think of characters on television or film who are poor speakers.

7 Mobile phones make it easier to speak to people.

8 People fall out a lot because of things that are said.

9 We can think of ten ways that speaking is used to get things done in our school.

10 If you are a good speaker, you talk loudly.

11 If you are a good speaker, you can talk for longer than anyone else.

12 If people are not talking, they have no ideas or are not interested.

13 Speaking helps us to learn.

Now think about learning in class and decide together on five things that go to make **a good speaker!**

Ask groups to think together about speaking in class, using **6.3 Talking Points: Speak up!** No need to write anything down.

Ask the whole class to discuss their responses to the Talking Points. You might want to concentrate on just a few; 9–13 are the most relevant to understand the importance of classroom talk.

A 'good speaker' can describe different ways of speaking, depending on the context. A good after-dinner speaker tells funny stories and holds the floor; a politician who is a good speaker may read a speech prepared by someone else. Neither would qualify as a good speaker in the context of a whole-class discussion, which requires listening and thoughtful, relevant contributions. Bring out what makes 'a good speaker' in your classroom, which is to do with learning and helping others to learn.

Ideas will vary, but a good speaker in class is able to speak:

- clearly

- adding detail or elaborating ideas

- with enthusiasm

- in a well-informed way

- thoughtfully

- by building on what others have said

- giving reasons for ideas and opinions

- offering helpful or probing questions

- giving sensible answers that lead to further questions

- in a way that shows they have been listening.

Explain the purpose of subsequent *speaking* activities:

- to make sure that everyone understands how and why to speak in class;

- to help everyone in the class to become a good speaker.

Reinforce this idea – that it is no use if only a few people in your class are wonderful speakers. We all need to learn to speak and listen effectively, otherwise those who do not may stop themselves and others learning. Also, everyone has a different combination of the skills that make 'a good speaker' and this is what each person can offer their classmates. For whole-class learning, each child has to make sure that everyone else knows how to speak clearly and confidently. It's a whole-class venture.

6.4 Speaking record

Child's name _____

Highlight, date and initial when these speaking skills have been used.

Contexts for speaking

describing	reading aloud	read own work	choral	poem
tell a story	with props	explain facts	explain ideas	given topic
present information	interview	perform	conversation	give opinions with reasons
argument	question	perform	conversation	discuss

Describing speaking

audible	clear	varied pace	emphasis	intonation
detailed	expressive	amusing	logical	understand-able
with meaning	volume	elaborate	effective	reasonable
answering questions	taking account of others	used ground rules	respectful	thoughtful
enthusiastic	serious	persuasive	responsive	amusing

Introduce the idea of evaluating (or judging or assessing) speaking as a way of ensuring that everyone is given supportive feedback on how they are getting on.

6.4 Speaking record provides a format for recording contexts and the details of progression which can be completed over time by the child, yourself and your teaching assistants.

A context for speaking activities: Honister Slate Mine

The next section provides examples of how a range of speaking and listening activities can be generated from one cross-curricular topic.

Honister Slate Mine provides a context for a range of activities focused on developing speaking skills and understanding. The Honister Slate Mine, between Buttermere and Borrowdale, is a remote and magical place in the Lake District fells.

For each session, share learning intentions with a focus on speaking. Use the PNS Speaking framework and resources **6.3** and **6.4** to help you to do this. Use plenary sessions to help children see their progress in speaking, ensuring that every child is encouraged to contribute and provide positive feedback for others. Record progress and experience using **6.4 Speaking record**.

6.5 Information: Honister Slate Mine provides notes for children about the mine, its history and the work done there. This is taken from the Honister Slate Mine web pages – 'a mine of wonderful resources!' – all of which can support the teaching of speaking and listening, as well as study of history, science and geography. The site provides high quality educational material for use with and by children.

Provide each group with a different paragraph. Use the information for speaking activities:

* Ask the group to prepare their text to read aloud.

* Ask groups to create a freeze frame with narrators, or a one-minute play to bring the text to life. Perform for the class and answer questions.

* Ask groups to make a brief PowerPoint or other presentation which emphasises key facts and vocabulary. Share with the class.

* Ask groups to create an annotated drawing which illustrates the text and includes all the information. Share this with the class.

6.5 Information: Honister Slate Mine

What is Honister slate?

About 45 million years ago, Honister was a volcanic area. Huge sheets of lava and rock were spread on the land. The earth was still forming, and these layers or beds of lava were buried under other layers of new rock. Tremendously high temperatures and enormous pressure changed the lava into slate. This sort of change, in which something new is made, is called metamorphosis. Slate is a metamorphic rock. There are three veins of slate at Honister, known as the Quey Foot, Honister, and Yewcrag or Kimberley Veins. They vary in thickness from about 4 to 14 m (13 to 45 ft). Honister Crag is 630 m (2,067 ft) high. Its grid reference is NY 212142.

What is it used for?

Honister slate is very hard and is of very high quality. Because it is weather-proof, it can be used for building. It varies in colour from a light sea green to dark blue-green and even a terracotta red, with some slate having bands of the different colours. Because it was formed in layers, slate can be split along these layers to make thin, hard, waterproof roofing tiles and paving stones. Honister slate is used for its durability and because it looks very attractive. Inside buildings, it is used for hearth-stones, work-tops and small items such as lamp bases and chopping boards.

What is the history of Honister Slate Mine?

Slate was mined from the Honister area in Roman times, and maybe even earlier. Monasteries built in the thirteenth century have slate roofs, and local buildings used slate for walls, floors and tiles. During the 1700s there was an open quarry, and from 1833 underground mining added to the output. During all this time the miners lit their way with tallow candles. The heavy slate was carried down the mountain by pack-horse, or by sleds with men running precariously down the steep slopes to the road. The railway reached Keswick in 1864 but there was still a mountain pass between the mine and the station, with horses and carts pulling the heavy slate. From about 1900 winding engines winched trucks downwards. Other transport methods were a tramway, an aerial ropeway (1928) and huge inclines inside the mountain (1930s).

Who works in the slate mines?

Early slate workers would have to walk for half a day through the mountains from Keswick, Whitehaven or Egremont to start work on Monday morning. During the week, some lived rough at Honister, often inside the mines. Some built bothies or shelters using the slate. These were very basic stone houses, with no water or furniture. They were unlikely to be either warm or dry. Here the miners stayed until their food ran out and their load of slate was ready to take down the mountain. Today, the journey from Keswick takes about half an hour by car or bus; it is still a dangerous road and motorists are warned to drive slowly.

6.5 Information: Honister Slate Mine *(continued)*

Mining the slate

Once the slate is sawn out of the seam, miners today carry out the same tasks as people have done for hundreds of years. These are:

Docking: Miners divide the large, sawn pieces (clogs) to a thickness of four slates (about 32 mm) ready to be rived. This docking, or cutting, is achieved with the use of a small chisel and a 21 lb mallet, cutting with the grain.

Riving: Once docked, the slate can be rived, by splitting the sections, again by hand, with a mallet and broad-bladed chisel, into four slices each. This produces slates which are a suitable thickness. (The width of the chisel equals the total thickness of eight finished slates.) Riving is carried out along the grain.

Dressing: Having made the slates the correct thickness, dressing is the process that cuts them into the precise shape required. A series of blades revolve and chop off the edges and corners of the material, leaving a completed slate, ready for use.

Slates are inspected, stacked in size order and packed for transport.

Saving the mine!

The Honister Slate Mine has always offered work for local people and produced slate – probably the hardest in the world – to be proud of. During the 1900s, the mine became run down and by 1986 it could no longer stay open. Many people were dismayed by its closure. But the mine re-opened eleven years later; if it had been derelict for another two years or so, it would have been too dangerous to ever re-open. The mine was saved thanks to the efforts of dedicated people whose ancestors had worked in the mine. They overcame many obstacles to keep the mine open, making sure that it did not damage the environment either for the wildlife or the many tourists who visit the Lake District National Park. They brought in new machinery, originally used to quarry marble in Italy. The mine now uses a combination of new expertise and the traditional methods to quarry and work the slate. Today, the mine sends slate all over the world. The motto of the mine owner who saved the mine is: 'It's better to have tried and failed than to have failed to try.' Luckily, and with much hard work, he succeeded.

Visiting the mine

Perhaps you might want to stay at Honister Hause Youth Hostel, the only other building near the mine at the top of the mountain pass. The Youth Hostel is a former quarry workers' building in a spectacular setting at the summit of Honister Pass, a high-level route connecting the valleys of Borrowdale and Buttermere. From here you can walk up the famous high peaks of Central Lakeland – Scafell, Great Gable, Pillar, Red Pike and Dale Head. You can visit the mine and watch the clogs of slate being sawn by huge machines. You can go on a tour of inside the workings. If you have an empty car boot, you can fill it with slate chippings for just £10. There are many slate items to look at and perhaps buy in the mine shop, and a café if you need refreshment. If you are very brave and adventurous, you can book to walk along the dangerous Via Ferrata or iron rope road to the top of Fleetwith Pike, a mountain 648 m (2,126 ft) high. Make it your ambition!

Speaking opportunities for group work: Honister Slate Mine

New words

Find new words about the slate mine (metamorphosis; rive; seam). Create a whole-class 'talking dictionary'; groups find out what one word means. In a whole-class session, explain the words in turn. Create a display of the new vocabulary, alphabetically on cards containing the vocabulary word and the group names, e.g. RIVE: Casey and James. Children can refer to these 'experts' for a definition at any time.

Describe

Ask groups in turn to describe the life of a slate miner, in Victorian times and today; how slate was formed; how slate was and is quarried, transported and used.

Read aloud

For example, using the Honister Mine web pages, read 'Transporting the slate' and use the discussion ideas suggested.

Choral speaking

Use **6.6 Ways into choral speaking**.

Tell a story

Prepare and orally tell the story of the life of Richard Brownrigg, 14-year-old miner; the story of the history of the mine; the story of a slate from volcano to roof; the story of a day on the mountain.

Explain

Prepare and explain how slate is formed as a rock, its properties and uses.

Present information

Collect and orally present (with PowerPoint/IWB) information about what slate can be used for; the colours of slate; a comparison of slate from different sources, e.g. Honister, Wales, Cornwall.

Perform

Mining, splitting and dressing the slate; building and living in a bothy in a rain storm; being a mine guide and showing a group of visitors around; debating whether to re-open the mine using **6.7 Who needs a slate mine?**

Sustain a conversation

- Ask groups to discuss ideas about the slate mine and the lives of miners.

- Discuss information presented on the mine's web site.

- Plan a journey to the Lake District and to Honister Pass.

- Look at and discuss information about the Via Ferrata and Richard Brownrigg.

- Discuss own experience of exciting and adventurous places.

- Prepare and share Talking Points about the mine.

Present a spoken argument

Use **6.7: Who needs a slate mine?**

Ask and answer questions

Ask groups to specialise in an aspect of the mine: its history, about slate, the miners' lives, the work of the miners, the shop and the mine today, the Via Ferrata, transporting slate, the landscape and weather in the Lake District. Find out what they can and create an information sheet or page. Devise an oral presentation. Organise opportunities for all groups to consider the work of other groups. While watching and listening, ask groups to think about what questions they can ask. Organise a question-and-answer session with each group taking a turn to answer their classmates' queries.

Discuss ideas, topics, issues

Using ground rules for exploratory talk, discuss:

- *Ideas*
    - a set of cartoons depicting the work of the miners
    - designing a house using slate
    - designing other items using slate (lamp stand, clock, barometer, paper weight, chopping board)
    - an adventure story based on visiting the mine.

- *Topics*
    - tourism in the Lake District.

- *Issues*
    - children at work, historically and present day
    - money values and wages.

Interviews

Create and role play interviews with the mine owner who re-opened the mine after eleven years of closure; with the person who runs the shop; with a mine tour guide; with a Roman miner; with Richard Brownrigg; and with someone who has actually visited the mine or used the Via Ferrata to find out how they felt.

6.6 Ways into choral speaking: Honister Slate Mine

Refrain: *Confident child or teacher speaks the solo; children say the refrain.*

Fleetwith Pike Rainstorm

Solo:	We are up near the sky and the rain hurtles down
Refrain:	We are up near the sky in the rain
Solo:	We are up near the sky and it's grey all around
Refrain:	We are up near the sky in the rain
Solo:	We are watching the water fly back to the ground
Refrain:	We are up near the sky in the rain
Solo:	We are miles from the shelter of village or town
Refrain:	We are up near the sky in the rain
Solo:	*(quietly, getting louder)* The waterfall drops past the cliff made of slate
	We are going to work and we must not be late
	We must get through the cloud to the sunlight again
Refrain:	*(enthusiastically)* We are up near the sky in the rain!

Antiphonal: *Class in two groups (A and B) who speak alternately.*

Working in the slate mine

A   What did you do at the slate mine today?
B   I sawed blocks of slate from the Kimberley Vein.
A   What did you do with the big clogs of slate?
B   With my mallet and chisel I docked on the grain.
A   What did you do with the docking complete?
B   With my broad bladed chisel I've riven the slate.
A   What did you do with the thin slabs of slate?
B   I dressed the stone ready to ship in a crate.

Line share: *An individual child, a pair or a group speak a line. All say the last two lines in unison. Ask children to write a second verse.*

Slate mine

Even now, there's a place too remote to be found
Where the light never reaches the rock underground
Up by Haystacks and Fleetwith, over Honister Hause,
Where the frost cracks the cliff and the peregrine calls,
In the mountain the vein's forty million years old,
Made of Buttermere slate, coloured deep sea-green gold.
Clock! Go the water drops, measuring time
On the scale of the mountains, in Honister mine.

6.6 Ways into choral speaking; Honister Slate Mine
(continued)

Unison: *All speak together in unison.*

Splitting slates

Tap Tap Tap Tap
(small group can repeat this throughout to keep rhythm)
Take the slate between your knees
Find the line to tap tap
Split the slate with greatest ease
Find the line to tap tap
Hold your chisel straight and true
Find the line to tap tap
Just a tap and that will do
Find the line to tap tap
Rive the slate and dress it round
Find the line to tap tap
Blue slates mined from underground
Find the line to tap!

Progression in choral speaking

- Listen to the words read aloud.

- Read the words of the poem silently.

- Read the words aloud individually.

- Read the words together with a group.

- Read the words aloud with the whole class.

- Learn the words and say aloud together.

- Think of and use appropriate expression, emphasis and rhythm.

- Perform for a range of audiences.

- Create own poems for choral speaking.

- Evaluate own performance and that of classmates.

6.7 Who needs a slate mine?

Group and whole-class discussion

Introduction: read the *context* for the discussion. Now divide the class into two: 'mine openers' and 'mine closers'. Provide groups with the relevant information paragraph. Ask children to read and discuss the information, and prepare to present it to the class. Everyone must speak; ensure that individual children think about what strong points they would like to make.

Context

It is 1990. Years of neglect and falling prices for slate have caused Honister Slate Mine to close down. Some people think this is a good idea. Others want to try to re-open it. Consider the *arguments* and *reasons* for both points of view.

(If possible, allow time and resources for further research into ideas and facts.)

The aim of the discussion is to *persuade* others in the group to see your point of view.

Mine closers

The mine is not making any money. No one lives nearby so it is impossible to find workers to do the mining. No one really knows how to dock and rive the slates any more. Young people don't want to be miners. It is a hard, dirty, dangerous job. There is no money in it. The slate is too expensive compared to modern building materials. Honister is not near any big railways or roads to move the slate. The slate has been taken from the easiest veins of slate, leaving only hard-to-get, expensive slate. No one is really interested in re-opening the mine. We could build a hotel and shopping centre here instead. Welsh slate is easier to quarry. The mine has been left so long that it is dangerous.

Mine openers

There are grants from the government that we can get because this is a heritage and tourist area, in the Lake District National Park. The mine will employ local people. Slate has been mined here for thousands of years and we must keep on this tradition. If we don't re-open the mine soon it will be so unsafe it will never open again. We can find people in Germany to show us how to mine and dress the slate. Honister Slate is the hardest and most attractive slate in the UK. Cumbrians are proud of their slate mine and want it open. People can travel to work here much more easily than they used to be able to. High quality buildings need our wonderful slate and some people can afford it.

Some ideas for the direct teaching of speaking

We expect children to speak out with their classmates listening; they may not want to, or may not know how to overcome their fear of doing so. They may refuse to speak if asked directly. We do ask children to share their most hypothetical and tentative ideas, sometimes with little or no preparation for what is in effect public speaking. The surprise is that when teachers ask questions, most children will have a go at answering, and are able to inform, explain or make their best guess clearly and confidently. But this leaves the less confident in an increasingly difficult position. They can tell that others are more capable when it comes to speaking. Their reluctance means that they may lose chances to practise their speaking skills and, having started off being a little quiet, they may feel self-conscious about what they say and how they say it if they do finally pluck up courage.

Children benefit from direct input about speaking in class. Terms which we use to describe how we speak, such as 'audibly', 'clearly' or 'with expression', can be better understood when examples are provided. Developing speaking skills becomes more relevant and motivating when reasons are given for the importance of clarity, articulate speech, expressive reading, and so on.

1 You can provide dedicated speaking lessons, or include learning intentions to do with speaking in other lessons where speech is a necessary part of learning or reporting on learning.

2 Decide on your speaking learning intention; for example: *'To be able to express your own ideas clearly when talking to your group'*. Explain what this means and model the language that children can use to express ideas, for example: *'my idea is'*; *'I think that'*. As a starter, provide such phrases on cards and ask the children to pass them round their group, reading the phrase before adding their idea.

3 Be explicit and talk about speaking skills; for example, clarity. How can this be achieved? Children might have their own ideas about who speaks clearly. Bring these out for discussion and give positive feedback to those who are nominated. Stress the importance of using straightforward language, asking questions that prompt talk and helping others to listen. Again, provide a model by offering an idea and asking children to re-phrase it. For example, offer an idea such as, 'I think that the most important thing in life is to have a lot of money'. Ask the children to talk about how this can be re-phrased, for example, 'I would like to be rich', or 'Money means a lot to me'. Do these mean exactly the same, or are there subtle differences?

4 In plenary sessions with *speaking* learning intentions, ask children to provide examples of their classmates who have achieved the intention.

5 Have speaking learning intentions in conjunction with curriculum intentions for each lesson during a whole week, then discuss the impact children feel this has had on their learning, their confidence, and their understanding of the importance of how and why they should speak clearly and confidently.

6 Teach children how to use external supports for speaking. Provide a PowerPoint presentation with picture slides on your topic. Ask groups to talk together to decide what they would say to accompany each slide. Each child is responsible for a slide, but the group helps to decide what to say. Practise by reading what will be said. Move on to talking with notes, then talking with no support but the slide. Talk about the transition from one slide to the next, from one speaker to the next. What phrases will help to hand over the talk, or to pick up from the previous speaker?

7 Ask children to think about speaking in different contexts – the classroom, assembly, with the head teacher, in the playground, at home, on the phone. What are the differences? Who gets nervous or anxious? Why, and what does it feel like? What strategies can help to get round such feelings? Bring out examples such as good preparation, making a list, rehearsal, taking a deep breath, a receptive audience.

8 Think about the physics of sound. Help children to understand the idea that sound begins at a source and is caused by vibration; that it travels through the air to reach our ears. Consider the physical aspects of sound using instruments to help children achieve an understanding of relevant vocabulary such as pitch, volume, tone, modulate, note, audible, clarity.

9 Help children to study the biology of how voices are produced. Draw and look at models of the vocal cords and describe their vibration, and the changes necessary to create different volumes and pitches. Relate this to the way the lungs provide air to move over the vocal cords, and the use of the diaphragm and intercostal muscles in breathing and speaking. Consider the effect of the jaw, teeth, tongue and soft palate on how sounds are formed. Can we use this knowledge to help us speak more clearly? Consider how the nervous system influences voice production. Think about singing. Look at how other animals – whales, cats, parrots – produce sound, and discuss the range of sounds that humans produce compared to other creatures.

10 Ask individuals to spend ten minutes *not speaking* and describe the effects on thinking and relating to others.

11 Help children to think about how sound is received in the ears and understood in the brain. Draw and describe how sound vibrates a gas – air, then solid – bone, then fluid – the inner ear – to create the conditions for hearing. Think how we look after our hearing and find out about what loud sounds do to ears over time.

12 Ask individuals to spend ten minutes wearing ear muffs and describe the effect on thinking and relating to others.

13 Help the class to think about oral language and its influence on our lives. Without speech, we find socialising and learning much more difficult. Ask bilingual children to talk about their experience of thinking and speaking, and describe the advantages and disadvantages they have found.

14 Make a class list poster. Show the children this and explain that each child in turn will be asked to speak in the plenary session, so that everyone has had the opportunity to speak and be heard. Names are crossed off or a tally compiled. Ask children to think about this idea and decide if they like it; why, or why not? What can the whole class do to encourage those who are not confident? What skills will everyone need to make this work well? Can these be directly taught? How does all this help learning?

15 Provide contexts in which children can practise projecting voices over distances. Can this be done without distortion? What difference do breath control and posture have on tone and volume? Can this be controlled? How can this help us to speak clearly and audibly in class and in other situations?

16 Think of ways to incorporate vocabulary to do with speaking into class lessons and activities. For example, speaking vocabulary includes:

    speak, say, tell, utter, pronounce, talk, declaim, discuss, recite, whisper, chatter, gossip, mumble, stutter, stammer, mutter, answer, converse, debate, interview, narrate, articulate, bilingual, clarity, confidence, intonation, vocabulary, interest, persuade – and, listen, actively.

Help the children to use such vocabulary in appropriate contexts and find opportunities to encourage them to use this developing understanding to describe, explain and analyse speech.

17 Speaking poetry.

Poems gain from being spoken aloud; learning proceeds from the process of preparing and performing a given poem, and listening to others do so. To move on to writing poems to be shared aloud is another benefit. As a way in to appreciating what poetry offers, groups or partners can prepare to read or speak from memory. This is also a chance to practise speaking before an audience and to listen to others, learning how to evaluate and provide constructive feedback.

You could start by getting out all your poetry books and asking every child to find a poem they like. The alternative is to provide poems, but this may not be quite as motivating – or surprising. Children can work with a partner to say what they like about their poem, then practise reading aloud to one another. Pairs join another group and listen to all of the poems in turn. They can prepare for whole-class work by deciding whether to read separate poems or share by taking stanzas of the same poem; deciding whether poems need sound effects, music or an introduction, and thinking how to say individual words, phrases and lines to create the best effect. Groups can read into a tape recorder or make an MP3 file, replay, evaluate and try again.

With the whole class as audience, perform the poems. Encourage children to say why they were chosen and be prepared to answer questions after the performance. Decide on another audience – younger children, parents, assembly, a parallel class – and organise a further performance, live or recorded.

Perhaps the children might go on to write their own poems for oral performance.

For another approach, see National Literacy Strategy Unit, Poetry Year 5, Term 3, *Choral and performance poems*.

18 Teach children how body language influences communication. For example, people are more likely to agree with you if you nod as you are speaking! Nodding does not really generate reasoned consensus or dialogue, but it has its uses as a way of helping someone to keep thinking through a problem, elaborate on an idea or recall difficult information. Similarly, arms folded across the chest, eye contact, yawning, looking at the floor or ceiling, tilting the head, all carry their own messages. It can be helpful to make some aspects of body language a little more explicit. However, children focusing their minds on this may find it hard to keep thinking about the subject under discussion, so there is a balance to be found between having never considered body language and being overly self-conscious about it.

19 Teach children how to give formative oral feedback about speaking, perhaps in the context of a story, poem, drama or reading. Ask children to listen to others and prepare to give them positive feedback. Display opening phrases and ask children to choose one which they would like to use to support a classmate's learning. Stress that children are to concentrate on pointing out how one of their classmates has achieved the learning intention or qualifies to be considered 'a good speaker'. Children should be aware that it is not their job to flag up problems. In this situation, criticism does much, but encouragement does more.

Summary

Speaking aloud in class is a perilous endeavour which most children tackle with admirable courage and fortitude. Children can benefit from direct instruction in various aspects of speaking in class. The whole class can take on the challenge of learning about why speaking is so important for us as social beings, and how to help others become articulate. Children can be taught to evaluate speaking, providing positive responses to the spoken words of others. Classroom contexts for learning can offer a range of opportunities for employing and extending speaking skills which are transferable to many other contexts.

Further reading

Collins, J. (1996) *The Quiet Child: Issues in Communication*. London: Continuum.

Goodwin, P. (2001) *The Articulate Classroom*. London: David Fulton Press.

Orme, D. and Andrew, M. (1997) *Speaking and Listening Curriculum Bank*. Leamington Spa: Scholastic.

Warren, C. (2004) *New Bright Ideas: Speaking and Listening Games*. Leamington Spa: Scholastic.

CHAPTER 7

Assessment

A straightforward assessment format for recording experience and progress

Speaking and listening Headline Objectives from the Literacy Framework for Years 3, 4, 5 and 6

1 Speaking

Most children learn to:

- speak competently and creatively for different purposes and audiences, reflecting on impact and response;

- explore, develop and sustain ideas through talk.

2 Listening and responding

Most children learn to:

- understand, recall and respond to speakers' implicit and explicit meanings;

- explain and comment on speakers' use of language, including vocabulary, grammar and non-verbal features.

3 Group discussion and interaction

Most children learn to:

- take different roles in groups to develop thinking and complete tasks;

- participate in conversations, making appropriate contributions building on others' suggestions and responses.

4 Drama

Most children learn to:

- use dramatic techniques, including work in role to explore ideas and texts;

- create, share and evaluate ideas and understanding through drama.

Speaking and listening assessment

7.1 Speaking and listening assessment record provides a basic resource for recording children's experience and attainment.

- Copy a sheet for each child. The boxes labelled 1–6 are for each half-term of a school year.
- Either tick, date, or colour (red, amber, green) to indicate attainment at the end of each half-term or when suitable.
- Add a note of the context or a reference to planning or any other record of the speaking and listening activity.
- The summary can be completed with the child and can include targets.

7.1 Speaking and listening assessment record

Name _____ Start date _____ End date _____

1 Speaking contexts

Objective	1	2	3	4	5	6	Summary
Speak competently and creatively for different purposes and audiences, reflecting on impact and response							
Explore, develop and sustain ideas through talk							

2 Listening and responding contexts

Objective	1	2	3	4	5	6	Summary
Understand, recall and respond to speakers' implicit and explicit meanings							
Explain and comment on speakers' use of language, including vocabulary, grammar and non-verbal features							

3 Group discussion and interaction contexts

Objective	1	2	3	4	5	6	Summary
Take different roles in groups to develop thinking and complete tasks							
Participate in conversations, making appropriate contributions building on others' suggestions and responses							

4 Drama contexts

Objective	1	2	3	4	5	6	Summary
Use dramatic techniques, including work in role to explore ideas and texts							

CHAPTER 8

Summary

Teaching speaking and listening enables the child to make the most of their education

Even now there are places where a thought might grow –
(A Disused Shed in Co. Wexford: Derek Mahon)

Children are taught through the medium of speaking and listening, but they also need to learn about the medium itself, if they are to use it well. Inattentive children distracted by one another's chatter may not know how and why to learn through speaking and listening; children required to be silent or to take part in question-and-answer guessing games may not realise the importance of active listening or the power of the spoken word. Making the skills of speaking and listening explicit, and discussing the thinking and learning that arises through talk, helps all children to become better involved in their own learning.

Class talk skills

Children learn from day one what is required of them as they turn into 'pupils'. They learn to sit in a certain way, to be quiet, to raise a hand when asked, and that there are certain ways to behave during particular sessions when teachers talk with them such as during whole-class work. Some children respond by lively interaction and open contribution. Some go quiet. Some drift off into a world of their own; some initiate distractions. But every child can be taught to understand the point and purpose of whole-class work, and their crucial role in it. They can recognise times when learning can take place through chances to generate common knowledge, and learn both how to take part and what the outcomes will be. Children can reflect on their contribution to what the class thinks, knows and understands, and begin to recognise that it is whole-class talk that helps to establish meanings. They can grow in understanding by being taught the skills they need to speak and listen in whole-class sessions. Motivation rises as they find satisfaction in thinking and learning with others.

Listening

Active listening is particularly important for learning before reading and writing are established and fluent, but it's easy to expect too much of young listeners. Children in class can seem to be learning because they are very amenable and quiet. But they listen only while they are interested – and the rest of the time they simply appear to listen. Superficially interactive questioning divides the class into those who will guess the answer and those who won't. Brevity, clarity and genuine questions are what teachers can aim for to ensure that children's attentiveness and curiosity are developed and put to good use. Teaching children how and why to listen to us and to each other provides them with insight into classroom life that helps them to make informed choices about behaviour. Children like to learn. Teaching them to reflect on the importance of listening generates interest in learning through the spoken word. The links between listening, thinking and speaking should be clear to every child.

Dialogic teaching

During dialogic teaching teachers and children think together, listening to each other, sharing ideas and bringing out a range of opinions and reasons. Children are confident enough to express emergent thoughts, aware that open sharing of ideas can generate joint understandings. Ideas are linked and examined, and give rise to further questions. Dialogic teaching is a way to talk about particular topics, but it also helps teachers and children to analyse and evaluate the effectiveness of discussion, making recommendations for future sessions. Classroom dialogue needs the teacher, with their clear vision and purposes for learning, as orchestrator. Teachers can provide children with excellent models for speaking and listening during dialogic whole-class sessions, generating whole-class exploratory talk. Dialogic teaching is the responsibility of the teacher for the benefit of the class.

Group work

Groups sharing a work space may work competitively or in parallel. At best, group work means that ideas are shared through talk. The difficulty for children is that their talk with others is dominated by social concerns. Group work puts relationships at stake; everyone is on thin ice. Other children are dominant, shy, unfriendly, off task or placidly agreeable; they shout, argue, ignore, rage, sulk or say nothing. However, every child can learn to transcend social effects by understanding why and how to take part in group discussion. This is not a set of innate skills and unless directly taught may never be part of a child's speaking and listening repertoire – much to their disadvantage in educational terms.

The educational importance of group talk only really becomes clear once the child has experience of exploratory talk and interthinking. How to discuss things can be taught by reasoning through the processes required to have 'a good discussion', and explaining the necessary skills and understanding. Being part of a working group that can use exploratory talk unaided by an adult is an intrinsically interesting learning situation, whatever the context for discussion. Children are supported in their efforts to achieve 'a good discussion' by deciding on mutual ground rules. The chance to analyse and evaluate the effectiveness of group talk, and its impact on joint understanding and learning, is also invaluable.

Speaking

Speaking aloud in class is such a problem for many children that they very rarely do it. Children who start off quiet when they arrive in school may get into a loop where their voice is never heard. If a quiet child speaks, it attracts attention; whether negative or positive, the child shrinks from it and resolves to be even quieter. Confident children may speak without a care for others. Disturbed children may share their anger and fear by speaking as they have been spoken to. Children need to know exactly what speaking is expected of them in a classroom. They must learn and experience the sort of speaking that helps everyone to learn. Crucially, they need to feel an atmosphere of trust and respect generated by all their classmates, a kind of amnesty that operates to ensure that all voices are heard without prejudice. We teachers can create the right environment by providing security, being a role model for children who have experienced little respect and trust, teaching explicit structures and language tools, and highlighting the small steps of progress as they happen. Speaking is a whole-class venture in which individual contributions reflect everyone's success in fostering an effective forum for thinking aloud.

Assessing speaking and listening

We may not be able to measure accurately children's social and emotional development; how they are coping with particular home circumstances; how they relate to other children and to adults; their developing interest in learning and knowing more about the world; their growing independence of mind, body and spirit; their attitudes towards the education they are offered and the uses they make of it. However, there are ways to see how children change over time, how their minds grow and their understanding of themselves in the world unfolds. 'Speaking and listening' is notoriously hard to assess and has been neglected as an area for teaching (but then so have science, physical exercise, music and art) in the push to – think about this phrase – 'drive up standards'. Standards are markers, often arbitrary, imposed on schools by those who see political capital in them. It is children and teachers who become driven. Now that the 'rise in standards' has peaked as teachers and children have become accustomed to a rigid learning and testing regime, how shall we respond? Is it time for another push on phonics, more summer schools for seven-year-olds, breakfast club top-ups and after-school SATs practice classes? Perhaps we can stop and take stock. What do we think education is for? What should it do for children? Teachers generally want to help children fulfil their potential, and work to raise the achievement of individuals and the attainment of the class. If we want children to become well socialised, make better sense of what happens around them, and contribute positively to their own lives and those of others, we must acknowledge that education has to pursue some immeasurable outcomes.

One aim of education for all teachers is to see children using talk to collaborate fully with others. This is because teachers have an overview of how children benefit when this happens. However, using talk to think together effectively needs constant input and practice. Luckily in school we have the right conditions – lots of children with lots to talk about – so we need not fail them by assuming that experience of 'a good discussion' will just happen as they go about their lives. We can and must make it happen in our classrooms.

The speaking and listening sections of the Literacy Framework offer a well structured and timely way forward, stressing how teaching and learning throughout the curriculum depends on spoken language. To make it work, we can provide children with direct tuition of speaking and listening; we can generate customised activities that support every child through inclusive discussion. We can utilise the power of dialogic teaching. Children can learn that talk is their best and most powerful tool for learning and for getting things done. This facility – the knowledge and understanding of how and why to engage in exploratory talk – is something that teachers can take great pride in helping young people to achieve. It offers children a way in to becoming literate, numerate, socially adept – and truly educated.

Further reading

Alexander, R. J. (2006) *Towards Dialogic Teaching: Rethinking Classroom Talk*, 3rd edition. York: Dialogos.

Baker, C. (2000) *A Parents' and Teachers' Guide to Bilingualism*. Clevedon: Multilingual Matters.

Barker, R. and Chapman, P. (2007) *Speaking and Listening Year 4: Photocopiable Activities for the Literacy Hour (Developing Literacy)*. London: A & C Black.

Barnes, D. (1992) *From Communication to Curriculum*. Portsmouth, NH: Boynton/Cook.

Barnes, D. and Todd, F. (1995) *Communication and Learning Revisited*. Portsmouth, NH: Heinemann.

Black, P., Harrison, C., Lee, C., Marshall, B., and Wiliam, D. (2004) *Working Inside the Black Box: Assessment for Learning in the Classroom*. London: NFER Nelson.

Blatchford, P., Kutnick, P. and Baines, E. (1999) *The Nature and Use of Classroom Groups*. Final Report, ESRC Project R000237255.

Bloom, B. S. (Ed.) (1956) *Taxonomy of Educational Objectives: The Classification of Educational Goals: Handbook I, Cognitive Domain*. New York/Toronto: Longmans, Green.

Clarke, S. (2001) *Unlocking Formative Assessment: Practical Strategies for Enhancing Pupils' Learning in the Primary Classroom*. London: Hodder & Stoughton.

Collins, J. (1996) *The Quiet Child: Issues in Communication*. London: Continuum.

Coultas, V. (2007) *Constructive Talk in Challenging Classrooms*. London: Routledge.

Cremin, T. (2007) Drama. In T. Cremin and H. Dombey (eds), *Handbook of Primary English in Initial Teacher Education*. Leicester: UKLA.

Cummins, J. (2000) *Language, Power and Pedagogy. Bilingual Children in the Crossfire*. Clevedon: Multilingual Matters.

Corden, R. (2000) *Literacy and Learning through Talk*. Buckingham: Open University Press.

Daniels, H. (2001) *Vygotsky and Pedagogy*. London: Routledge.

Dawes, L., Wegerif, R. and Mercer, N. (2004) *Thinking Together: A Programme of Activities for Developing Speaking, Listening and Thinking Skills for Children Aged 8–11*. Birmingham: Questions Publishing.

DfES (2003) *Speaking, Listening, Learning: Working with Children in Key Stage 1 and 2*. London: HMSO.

Edwards, D. and Mercer, N. (1987) *Common Knowledge: The Development of Understanding in the Classroom*. London: Methuen.

Edwards, S. (1999) *Speaking and Listening for All*. London: David Fulton Publishers.

EMASS (2004) *Supporting Pupils with English as an Additional Language*. Milton Keynes: Milton Keynes Council, 1 Saxon Gate East, MK9 3HG.

Fernandez Cardenas, J. M. (2004) The Appropriation and Mastery of Cultural Tools in Computer-Supported Literacy Practices, Ph.D. thesis, Open University, Milton Keynes.

Fullan, M. (1982) *The Meaning of Educational Change*. London: Teachers College Press.

Galton, M. (2007) *Learning and Teaching in the Primary Classroom*. London: Sage.

Goodwin, P. (2001) *The Articulate Classroom*. London: David Fulton Press.

Grugeon, E., Hubbard, L., Smith, C. and Dawes, L. (2001) *Teaching Speaking and Listening in the Primary School*, 2nd edition. London: David Fulton Press.

Hadfield, J. and Hadfield, C. (2006) *Simple Listening Activities*. Oxford: Oxford University Press.

Howe, C. and Tolmie, A. (2003) Group Work in Primary School Science: Discussion, Consensus and Guidance from Experts. *International Journal of Educational Research*, 39(1–2): 51–72.

Mercer, N. (1995) *The Guided Construction of Knowledge*. Clevedon: Multilingual Matters.

Mercer, N. (2000) *Words and Minds*. London: Routledge.

Mercer, N. and Littleton, K. (2007) *Dialogue and the Development of Children's Thinking*. London: Routledge.

Mercer, N. Wegerif, R. and Dawes, L. (1999) Children's Talk and the Development of Reasoning in the Classroom. *British Educational Research Journal*, 25(1): 95–111.

NCC (1991) *Thinking, Talking and Learning in Key Stage Two*. York: National Curriculum Council.

Naylor, S. and Keogh, B. (2000) *Concept Cartoons in Science Education*. London: Millgate House Publishers.

O'Keefe, V. P. (1999) *Developing Critical Thinking: The Speaking and Listening Connection*. Portsmouth, NH: Heinemann.

Orme, D. and Andrew, M. (1997) *Speaking and Listening Curriculum Bank*. Leamington Spa: Scholastic.

Rockett, M. and Percival, S. (2002) *Thinking for Learning*. Stafford: Network Educational Press.

Rose, J. (2006) *Independent Teaching of Early Reading*. Nottingham: DfES.

Säljo, R. (1979) *Learning in the Learner's Perspective: Some Common Sense Conceptions*. Report from Department of Education, University of Groteborg, 76.

Sams, C., Wegerif, R., Dawes, L. and Mercer, N. (2004) *Thinking Together with ICT & Primary Mathematics*. London: Smile Mathematics.

Vygotsky, L. S. (1994) Extracts from *Thought and Language* and *Mind in Society*. In B. Stierer and J. Maybin (eds), *Language, Literacy and Learning in Educational Practice*. Clevedon: Multilingual Matters/Open University.

Wallace, B. and Bentley, R. (2002) *Teaching Thinking Skills Across the Middle Years*. London: David Fulton Press.

Warren, C. (2004) *New Bright Ideas: Speaking and Listening Games*. Leamington Spa: Scholastic.

Wertsch, J. V. (2002) *Voices of Collective Remembering*. Cambridge: Cambridge University Press.

Whitebread, D. (ed.) (2000) *The Psychology of Teaching and Learning in the Primary School*. London: Routledge.

Web links

Authors: Videos of authors talking about their books; resources about children's fiction. www.randomhouse.co.uk/childrens/home.htm

Behaviour 4 learning: Resources for classroom management. www.behaviour4learning. ac.uk/

British Library Sound Archive (Click 'listen'.) www.bl.uk/collections/sound-archive/ nsa.html

British Telecom: BT's Education programme based on communication. www.bteducation. org/

Concept Cartoons: Thought-provoking resources for discussion. www.conceptcartoons. com/index_flash.html

DfES: Inclusion – guided speaking and listening to support language development. www. standards.dfes.gov.uk/primary/publications/inclusion/bi_children/pri_pubs_bichd_ 214006_09.pdf

DfES: Speaking, Listening, Learning. www.standards.dfes.gov.uk/primary/publications/ literacy/818497/

DfES: Papers for Learning and Teaching. www.standards.dfes.gov.uk/primaryframeworks/ literacy/Papers/learningandteaching/

DfES: Planning for children learning English as an Additional Language. www.standards. dfes.gov.uk/primaryframeworks/downloads/PDF/EAL_Planning.pdf

DfES: Primary Framework for Literacy and Mathematics. www.standards.dfes.gov.uk/ primaryframeworks/

DfES: SEAL Social and emotional aspects of learning. www.standards.dfes.gov.uk/ primary/publications/banda/seal/

Dialogic Teaching: Dialogic teaching is an approach to teaching that, in a highly disciplined fashion, harnesses the power of talk to stimulate and extend pupils' thinking and advance their learning and understanding. www.robinalexander.org. uk/dialogicteaching.htm

Dialogic Teaching and Children's Talk: ICT resources to stimulate group discussion. www.dialogbox.org.uk/ICT.htm

Honister Slate Mine: 'A mine of useful resources!' www.honister-slate-mine.co.uk/ honister_slate_mine.asp

Learning and Teaching: Comprehensive information on theory and practice. www. learningandteaching.info/index.htm

Literacy Trust: Supporting the improvement of literacy skills. www.literacytrust.org.uk/ index.html

Mind Friendly Learning: All about thinking for learning ('Custom Pages'). www.school-portal.co.uk/GroupHomepage.asp?GroupID=91541

Playing Out: The Good Childhood Survey asks for children's opinions. http://sites. childrenssociety.org.uk/mylife/home.aspx

Quiet Child: Ways to help the 1 in 5 with 'communication apprehension'. www.jamesc mccroskey.com/publications/92.htm

Thinking Together: A talk-focused approach to thinking and learning. www.thinking together.org

Index